the GOSPEL according to ST. JOHN

HERALD SCRIPTURAL LIBRARY
Robert J. Karris O.F.M., General Editor

the GOSPEL according to ST. JOHN

A Theological Commentary

by

Pheme Perkins

FRANCISCAN HERALD PRESS
1434 WEST 51st STREET • CHICAGO, 60609

Library of Congress Cataloging in Publication Data

Perkins, Pheme.
　　The Gospel according to St. John.

　　(Herald scriptural library)
　　Bibliography: p.
　　1. Bible. N.T. John—Commentaries. I. Title.
BS2615.3.P47　　226'.5'07　　77-12896
ISBN 0-8199-0687-5

NIHIL OBSTAT:
　　Mark Hegener O.F.M.
　　Censor

IMPRIMATUR:
　　Msgr. Richard A. Rosemeyer, J.C.D.
　　Vicar General, Archdiocese of Chicago

November 28, 1977

"The Nihil Obstat and the Imprimatur are official declarations that a book or pamphlet is free of doctrinal and moral error. No implication is contained therein that those who have granted the Nihil Obstat and Imprimatur agree with the contents, opinions, or statements expressed."

Abbreviations

The Old Testament

Genesis	Gn	Proverbs	Prv
Exodus	Ex	Ecclesiastes	Eccl
Leviticus	Lv	Song of Songs	Song
Numbers	Nm	Wisdom	Wis
Deuteronomy	Dt	Sirach	Sir
Joshua	Jos	Isaiah	Is
Judges	Jgs	Jeremiah	Jer
Ruth	Ru	Lamentations	Lam
1 Samuel	1 Sm	Baruch	Bar
2 Samuel	2 Sm	Ezekiel	Ez
1 Kings	1 Kgs	Daniel	Dn
2 Kings	2 Kgs	Hosea	Hos
1 Chronicles	1 Chr	Joel	Jl
2 Chronicles	2 Chr	Amos	Am
Ezra	Ezr	Obadiah	Ob
Nehemiah	Neh	Jonah	Jon
Tobit	Tb	Micah	Mi
Judith	Jdt	Nahum	Na
Esther	Est	Habakkuk	Hb
1 Maccabees	1 Mc	Zephaniah	Zep
2 Maccabees	2 Mc	Haggai	Hg
Job	Jb	Zechariah	Zec
Psalms	Ps(s)	Malachi	Mal

The New Testament

St. Matthew	Mt	1 Timothy	1 Tm
St. Mark	Mk	2 Timothy	2 Tm
St. Luke	Lk	Titus	Ti
St. John	Jn	Philemon	Phlm
Acts of the Apostles	Acts	Hebrews	Heb
Romans	Rom	St. James	Jas
1 Corinthians	1 Cor	1 St. Peter	1 Pt
2 Corinthians	2 Cor	2 St. Peter	2 Pt
Galatians	Gal	1 St. John	1 Jn
Ephesians	Eph	2 St. John	2 Jn
Philippians	Phil	3 St. John	3 Jn
Colossians	Col	St. Jude	Jude
1 Thessalonians	1 Thes	Revelation	Rv
2 Thessalonians	2 Thes		

Non-Biblical Ancient Writings

JEWISH

(a) Old Testament Pseudepigrapha
   (Can be found in R. H. Charles, *Aprocrypha and Pseudepigrapha of the Old Testament.* New York: Oxford, 1963†)

2 Bar	Second Baruch
4 Ez	Fourth Ezra
Jub	Jubilees
PsSol	Psalms of Solomon
T. Jud.	Testament of Judah
T. Lev.	Testament of Levi

(b) Dead Sea Scrolls
   (Can be found in A. Dupont-Sommer, *The Essene Writings from Qumran.* New York: World (Meridian), 1962.)

1 QpHab	Commentary on Habakkuk
1 QM	Scroll of the War Rule
1 QS	Scroll of the Rule

(c) Rabbinic and other Jewish writings
   (Josephus and Philo are included in the volumes of the *Loeb Classical Library*)

Josephus, Ant.	Josephus, Antiquities of the Jews
Josephus, War	Josephus, The Jewish War
MidMekiltaExodus	Midrash Meklta on Exodus
MidRabLam	Midrash Rabbah on Lamantations
confus ling	Philo, On the Confusion of Tongues
de somn	Philo, On Dreams
T. B. Griffin	Babylonian Talmud, Tractate Griffin
T. B. San	Babylonian Talmud, Tractate Sanhedrin

EARLY CHRISTIAN WRITERS

(These may be found in collections of early Christian writers such as *The Ante-Nicene Fathers;* the apocryphal gospels may be found in E. Hennecke & W. Schneemelcher, *New Testament Apocrypha,* Philadelphia: Westminster, 1963.)

CG	Cairo Gnostic Codices (a collection of Gnostic writings also known as the Nag-Hammadi Codices, an English translation is to be published by Harper & Row in 1978)
con Cel	Origen, Contra Celsum
Did	Didache (found among the Apostolic Fathers, which are also in the Loeb Classical Library)
GPet	Gospel of Peter
GTh	Gospel of Thomas
Ignatius, Phila	Ignatius of Antioch, To the Philadelphians (Apostolic Fathers)
Ignatius, Rom	Ignatius of Antioch, To the Romans
Justin, Apol	Justin Martyr, Apology
Justin, Dial	Justin Martyr, Dialogue with Trypho

Introduction

Debate and controversy are not only reflected in the text of the Fourth Gospel, they have attended its interpretation ever since it was written. Why is it so different from the other gospels? Even the casual reader can see that the picture of Jesus drawn in its pages is quite unlike the others'. The parables, full of details of life in first-century Palestine, and the short, memorable sayings have all but vanished. Instead, Jesus engages in dialogues that are loaded with irony and double-meaning. He delivers long discourses whose symbolism can only become intelligible to the Christian, who has read the whole gospel through. In place of the short anecdotes of the synoptic tradition, we find great religious symbols: life, light, the shepherd, the way, and even the divine I AM. The other gospels open either at the beginning of Jesus' ministry or at his birth; John begins with the presence of the divine Word with the Father at creation. Even the miracles, which John calls "signs," point beyond themselves to the great symbols of vine, light, and life. The constant use of symbolic language gives the Fourth Gospel a quality of universality and timelessness that has endeared it to mystics and poets throughout the centuries.

At the same time, the language of the gospel is what a modern anthropologist would call *emic;* that is, it is a language of contrasts and clarifications that has been built up within a small community. *Emic* language is contrasted with *etic,* that is, that language of science and scholarship, which tries to be universally accessible and value-free. The language of the Fourth Gospel is so clearly that of a particular faith community that we may not even be sure that it would be properly understood by first-century outsiders, who

ix

used similar symbols. When we use other first-century writings to help us understand the connotations of the language John is using, we must constantly be alert for changes and nuances introduced by the Johannine tradition.

In that spirit, much of our analysis is devoted to setting the gospel within its historical context. That endeavor first demands that we attend to the linguistic background of the Evangelist. What could his words and symbols have meant to his first-century readers? Not surprisingly, the very universality of those symbols has led to heated debates over the correct interpretation of the Fourth Gospel. Some interpreters understand John against the background of one of the Graeco-Roman religious traditions, pagan mysticism, or Gnosticism, while others trace the same symbolic language in the Old Testament and in Jewish writings contemporary with the gospel. (One scholar has even tried to argue that John was influenced by contemporary Buddhist thought!) Despite such disparate views, recent studies of the Fourth Gospel have made great progress in using Jewish writings from the same period to elucidate not only the language but the style of argument in the gospel. Written from that perspective, this commentary utilizes the results of that research to show that the Evangelist was seriously engaged in defending Christian claims about Jesus against Jewish objection.

The gospel itself contains hints that the dialogue with Judaism had brought severe consequences for members of its community. We are told that some people will not admit to believing in Jesus because they are afraid of being put out of the synagogue—a penalty the Jews enacted against the Christians around A.D. 90. Further, the disciple is told to expect persecution from the synagogue; he or she may even be put to death for religious reasons (16:1–4a). The severity of the argument between Jesus and his Jewish opponents in these pages may indicate the extreme difficulty into which the community of John's day had been cast. They must learn from him how to defend their belief that Jesus is the Son of God and the only way to salvation against charges that such claims were both blasphemous and clear violations of God's revelation in the Old Testament.

The second area in which the context of this gospel is becoming clearer because of recent research is its relationship to earlier Christian traditions. The Evangelist has not worked out this unusual narrative *ex nihilo*. Scholars find increasing evidence that he used a variety of traditional materials. Detailed comparison with the synoptic tradition suggests that he knew stories of the life of Jesus that were similar to that tradition but independent of it—and in some cases perhaps even earlier versions of an incident. Even where there are no synoptic parallels, literary and form-critical analysis has helped us see that the Evangelist is relying on earlier tradition. Sometimes, he seems to be quoting the creeds and liturgy of his own community.

But the Evangelist is not just collecting old traditions and answering Jewish charges. He has addressed himself to the problems of his community and used the tradition in such a way as to present new and creative expressions of Christian faith. Thus he has earned the title "theologian" that is so often given him in the Fathers. The primary aim of this commentary is to help Christians of today appreciate the exciting and creative dimensions of the Evangelist as theologian by showing how he worked with his tradition.

Sometimes ancient and modern readers have found the picture of Jesus presented in John too one-sided. He is so divine that the human seems swallowed up by the Word. They miss the "homey" touches of the parables, which seem to speak more directly to the lives of common people than to the great, universal symbols of the Fourth Gospel. Some have even implied that his stress on the divinity of Jesus denies his real humanity.

Our analysis of the controversy dialogues in the gospel suggests that Christian belief in the divinity of Jesus was under challenge. If the gospel stresses Jesus' unity with the Father, it is to safeguard the Church's confession against its opponents that Jesus is Son of God, not to expound a heretical Christology against other Christians. Further, the Evangelist's use of tradition shows that he presupposes readers who knew those traditions about Jesus. The gospel was not intended to be their first introduction to or their only source of knowledge about him. Rather, John's readers would find familiar stories and parts of the liturgy retold from a new perspective.

Because he focuses so much on Jesus and on individuals, John has also been read as a highly individualistic and eccentric work. But as we proceed with our analysis we find that he is constantly addressing the needs of the larger community of believers. The abiding presence of the risen Lord is found only within that community. For him, as for any New Testament author, theological reflection is not a solo performance. It is guided by the traditions, needs, and problems of the Church in a particular time and place. The Evangelist sees that activity as part of the permanent legacy given the Church, when the risen Jesus sent the Paraclete.

Although we show how the Evangelist was a creative and exciting theologian in his own day, we would not be true to his legacy if we did not reflect on how his vision might speak to our own theological concerns. In short compass, we can hardly do justice to the theological suggestiveness of a work which has inspired the rock musical *Jesus Christ Superstar,* the Christology of Bishop J. A. T. Robinson, and many of the great mystics. But at certain points we step out of our role as historical exegete to ask how the Evangelist might address some of our contemporary preoccupations. His insistence that the theologian must evaluate and reformulate what he or she takes over from the surrounding culture in the light of God's revelation in Jesus may be a salutary anecdote to "pop-theologizing." We may feel that we have not yet come around to really reflecting upon the views which he paints as central to Christian faith: that God is revealed in Jesus; that Jesus is savior for *all peoples* —not just those of western European descent; that a person must be confronted with the message of Jesus in such a way that he or she is challenged to decide either for or against His word; that Jesus continues to be represented in the world by the community he established. All these topics make present-day Christians uneasy. They are no longer sure what to say when such questions are raised. Lay people who read a draft of this book consistently picked out those questions as the ones about which they felt most confusion when they found themselves talking about their religion to others. Their reaction shows how badly we need a responsible theological apologetics for the church of our day—just as the evangelist did for his. A commentary such as this one cannot fill that need, but we may hope that the evangelist's example and the continued guidance of the Spirit will inspire some to such efforts.

Contents

Part Four
CRUCIFIXION/RESURRECTION: THE GLORIFICATION OF JESUS

PART ONE
Calling Disciples

1. Jesus, the Divine Word

The first chapter of John introduces Jesus as the Word of God. The reader of the gospel knows from the outset that Jesus can be identified with God, that he is greater than all other religious figures, and that he is the only salvation possible for the world. The author also makes it clear that many people will reject the claims made for Jesus. Therefore, he builds the second half of the chapter around a series of conversion stories which show how a person should respond to the message about Jesus. Each one follows up what he is told about Jesus by going to Jesus personally and finding out that he is even more than what had been said about him. Sometimes that process demands that an individual come to a new realization about himself. These stories highlight a theme that occurs many times in this gospel. Jesus confronts people with a decision they cannot escape, and either they will accept him as light of the world or they will be condemned to darkness; there is no middle ground. The gospel abounds in symbols which make the same point: light/darkness, life/death, salvation/judgment, from above/from below.

John 1:1–18 *Prologue: the Divine Word*

Unlike the other gospels, John opens with creation. Its first words, "In the beginning," are also the first words of the Greek Old Testament. This setting typifies much of the language of the Fourth Gospel. Its many cosmic symbols often give the narrative an aura of timelessness. The prologue incorporates an early Christian hymn to Jesus as the

divine Word. This Word has both created the world and revealed God to us. Colossians 1:15-20 quotes another early
hymn which described Christ's role in both creation and
redemption. Such hymns show that as Christians reflected on
Christ's exaltation as Redeemer they came to see him as
active in the world since its beginning. The Evangelist does
not separate the words of the hymn from his own comments
on it, so we cannot always be sure where one begins and the
other ends. However, there is general agreement that at
least the following verses came from the hymn: 1-4; 5 or
9ab; 10-11; 12a(?); 14a, b(?), c; and 16.

The opening stanza of the hymn describes the role of the
divine Word in creation and as a source of life and guidance
for humanity. But we are reminded that people do not
always accept the light of that divine Word (v. 5). Later
in the gospel, the image of light will be used for the ministry
of Jesus. People will also reject his light (Jn 12:35-36).

Redemptive Activity of the Word

Before he describes the redemptive activity of the divine
Word, the Evangelist injects a passage on John the Baptist's
role as a witness to the Word (vv. 6-8). John has several
references to the Baptist which stress his subordination to
Jesus. Throughout the gospel he testifies openly to Jesus'
divine origin and mission. The evangelist constantly reminds
us that faith comes through the testimony of others: the
Father testifies to Jesus, Jesus testifies about his Father, and
people testify to their faith in Jesus (also see v. 15).

Some scholars think that verses 9-13 refer to the activity
of the Word prior to the incarnation, for example, in the
Old Testament. Others point out that since the Evangelist
has put this section after John the Baptist, he must under-

stand it as a description of Jesus' ministry. His comment on this section (vv. 12c–13) bears out that view. He contrasts the adoption of believers as children of· God with the rejection of the Word by "his own," the Jews. John 3:3–8 describes the Spirit as making "rebirth" possible. Thus John has in mind the new people of God, brought into being through baptism.

The final section of the hymn (vv. 14 and 16) speaks of Jesus' incarnation in language reminiscent of Old Testament descriptions of God's glory dwelling among his people (see Jl 3:17, Ez 43:7). The phrase "grace and truth" (v. 14) probably translates the Hebrew expressions *hesed* (mercy) and *emeth* (truth), which refer to God's graciousness in making a covenant with his people and his absolute fidelity to the promises of that covenant. Therefore, the NAB has translated these words as "enduring love." Verse 16 concludes with the difficult phrase "grace for grace" (NAB translates it "love following upon love"). It probably refers to the new grace associated with Jesus' revelation.

The Evangelist interprets these verses of the hymn by contrasting the two covenants. Jesus not only brings the love which the Old Testament associates with the revelation to Moses (v. 17) but he brings true revelation, because he is himself the revelation of God (v. 18). This verse claims that Jesus is superior to Moses, since the latter did not see God (Ex 33:18). The glory of the only Son is seen by the believer (cp. 1 Jn 1:1f.). Many of these themes recur throughout the gospel, which stresses the unique relationship between Jesus and the Father.

The Word

The prologue to the Fourth Gospel identifies Jesus as the

divine Word *(logos)*. The universality of that symbol has given it a long and fruitful history in Christian theology; but that same universality poses difficulties for the interpreter. "Word" was an important philosophical and religious concept in two quite different settings, and exegetes are divided as to which context underlies the Johannine usage.

Greek philosophical tradition from the pre-Socratic Heraclitus through the Stoics identified the rational, ordered unity of the universe as "word." Stoic philosophers spoke of that "word" as divine. Graeco-Roman religious thinkers often used philosophical concepts to provide a reasonable interpretation of ancient myths. The Jewish philosopher, Philo, made extensive use of Stoic and Platonic ideas in interpreting the Old Testament. In his philosophical interpretation of the creation stories, Philo speaks of two divine "words." One, the "elder son," is the conception of the new world which God has eternally in his mind, the noetic universe. The other, the "younger son," is the agency through which God creates and orders the visible universe. Although the Old Testament provided a basis for saying that God created the cosmos through his "word," Philo's account is clearly indebted to philosophical principles of cosmogony and theology. A divine hypostasis, which can be the subject of a verb, has replaced the activity of God, who creates by "speaking"—an activity too anthropomorphic for a supreme being, which must be the "eternal one" of the philosophers.

Other examples of the use of a hypostasized divine word in a creation account may be found in the popular revelations of the *Corpus Hermeticum*, especially the first tractate, known as the *Poimandres*, where "the word" figures in a highly eclectic mythological account which combines ancient Near Eastern cosmogonic images with language from the Greek translation of Genesis and philosophical terminology. Some interpreters (see Dodd, *Interpretation*, pp. 263–84) think that John was drawing upon such popular philosophy. Certainly a person who came to Christianity with that background could read the prologue to the gospel as claiming that Jesus embodies everything which such myths claimed to reveal. But it seems to us unlikely that the prologue was composed on the basis of such traditions. Unlike other writings—pagan, Jewish and, later, Christian, which use philosophical language to expound ancient myths—John does not employ a technical philosophical vocabulary.

Therefore, others (see Schnackenburg, 1:481-93; Brown, 1:519-24) insist that the Old Testament provides the context for understanding the Johannine use of "Word." There, "word of God" is a fundamental metaphor for describing the relationship between God and humanity. Revelation is based on the analogy with hearing something, rather than with seeing God or a vision. The phrase "word of God" embraces the whole revelation through Moses and the prophets, and that revelation demands obedience. It can also be used for God's creative activity. Psalm 119 is a meditation on the word of God which illustrates its varied meanings. This psalm associated the word of God with light, life, and truth—all important Johannine symbols for the revelation of God in Jesus. The Jewish traditions about the "wisdom" of God developed a picture of wisdom as God's agent in creation and revelation (see Prv 8, Wis 7-9). Those who receive wisdom are said to become friends of God (Wis 7:27). John's picture of the Word as a personified agent of God in creation and revelation—making people "children" of God—seems to be indebted to such wisdom traditions.

The prologue to the gospel is the only place where we find the Word described in this cosmic sense. It is the only place where Jesus is said to be the Word. The rest of the book either uses "word" in its purely secular meaning of word, statement, or discourse (2:19-22, 4:39, 12:38, 15:25) or with its religious meaning as God's message or commandment (5:24, 8:31, 17:14). In the latter case, Jesus is the sole bearer of that revelation and thus may be seen in the narrative to be acting as Word. When John calls Jesus "Word," then, he is not saying something about a peculiar, inhuman nature possessed by Jesus; he is describing his function as the unique source of revelation about God.

This usage points to another very important fact about John's use of symbols. Their conceptual background and use elsewhere in the religious language of the first century never tells the whole story. All of John's symbolic language is Christological. It expresses the universality of Jesus' mission. The paradox of Jesus' divinity, universality, and unique relationship to the Father will dominate much of the narrative. The references to the incarnation in verses 14 and 16 and the passages on John the Baptist prepare the reader for the coincidence of universality and particularity, the divine and a specific human individual, which makes the message about Jesus so difficult to comprehend. Briefly, John's use of "word" illustrates three important characteristics of his symbolic language. First, it has a Jewish matrix, which can be traced in the Old Testament and other contemporary Jewish writings. Second, it also has a more universal application, so that it can be tied to the other religious and philosophical traditions of the Evangelist's time. Third, it is specifically Christological. Such symbols as word, light, and life not only reveal the universality of Jesus' mission—he is Savior of the world—but they are determined and redefined by his own particularity. A Johannine symbol is never simply taken over in its old meaning; it has always been reformulated in light of the new revelation.

Symbolic discourse makes it possible to express several concepts and allusions at once. Johannine symbols tend to be applicable to a wide diversity of religious and cultural contexts, although the precise associates of a given symbol will vary with its context. "Word," for example, is a fundamental human experience. Every human being learns to hear and respond. The portrayal of Jesus as Word of God remains accessible even in cultures where more particular images, such as that of Jesus as shephard, are not part of people's experience. At the same time, we must watch out for a reading of such symbols which would reduce Jesus to our common experience of word, life, or light. Those symbols are clues to the salvation made possible by Jesus' revelation, but he is greater than any of them, as the Evangelist will make clear.

John 1:19–51 *The Witness to Jesus*

The prologue introduced John the Baptist as a witness to the light coming into the world; now the narrative embodies that affirmation. The Baptist consistently refuses to accept any messianic titles for himself and openly designates Jesus as the expected Messiah. His testimony will provide Jesus with his first disciples. The Evangelist stresses the necessity of testimony in bringing people to Jesus. He also uses language about testimony and witnesses throughout the gospel as part of a legal metaphor of trial and judgment which describes the relationship between Jesus and the world. His testimony about the Father calls the world to judgment. At the same time, those who reject Jesus are constantly judging him and demanding witnesses for the claims he makes. John understands the mission of the Christians as carrying that testimony to the world. Their testimony has to be about Jesus. Thus he presents John the Baptist as a model.

These opening stories introduce the major Jewish designa-

tions for figures who were expected to come and to in-
augurate the new age: messiah (christ), Elijah, the prophet,
lamb of God, son of God, king of Israel, son of man.
Jews used a variety of images and metaphors to describe
the salvation they expected God to bring to Israel. This
variety shows that there was no standard picture of the
person or persons who would act on God's behalf in inau-
gurating the new age. Since Christians believe that Jesus
has fulfilled that role, they use those titles and metaphors
to describe him. The first chapter of John combined two of
our main sources for early Christological beliefs, a Christological hymn and the messianic titles used for Jesus, in its
opening presentation. Both the divinity of Jesus, as it was
expressed in the hymn, and his claim to fulfill and even
transcend Jewish messianic expectation will be the topic of
public controversy throughout the rest of the gospel.

The Baptist Is Questioned

The narrative half of Chapter 1 is built around paired
episodes. Here (vv. 19–28), the Baptist is questioned about
his identity and mission by two groups: first by priests and
Levites sent by some Jews from Jerusalem, then by some
people sent by the Pharisees. We will find this dual-scene
structure used frequently in the Fourth Gospel; it seems to
be one of the literary techniques of the author. Thus in
this passage he seems to have created a double story, from
one which originally had only one set of questioners, by
adding the references to those who were sent by the Pharisees.

When questioned about his identity, the Baptist denies
that he fulfills any of the expected messianic roles. He is
not the Messiah. Compare Luke 3:5, where the Baptist
counters belief that he may be the Messiah by referring to

the fire-baptism of the one who comes after him. He is not Elijah. Contrast Mark (1:2, 8:13) and Matthew (11:14, 17:12), where John is the fulfillment of that expectation (based on Mal 3:1). He is not the prophet, as Moses predicted in Dt 18:15ff. He is merely the voice of one crying in the wilderness (Is 40:3). This Isaiah quotation is used of the Baptist in the synoptic accounts, though the citation of the Old Testament in John—as is usual with his OT citations (see Dodd, *Interpretation,* p. 252)—is independent of the synoptic form of the citation. This elaborate series of denials reflects the view already voiced in the prologue: John is not the light but merely a witness to it. The care the Evangelist has given to detailing the proper relationship between the Baptist and Jesus suggests that Christians were still being challenged by those who claimed a messianic or prophetic role for the Baptist.

As in the synoptics, a discussion of the difference between John's baptist (water) and that of the Christians (spirit) follows upon the presentation of the Baptist as the voice. The second episode centers on the legitimacy of John's baptism, given that he has no messianic title. The Evangelist does not contrast the two types of baptism, as one might expect from the synoptics. He knows the tradition about Jesus' spirit-baptism (see 1:33) and, therefore, seems to have chosen not to use it in his account (compare the denial that Jesus baptized in 4:2). Instead, he concentrates on the status of the two figures. The traditional saying about John's unworthiness to undo Jesus' sandal is combined with allusions to 1:15, 30, where Jesus' superiority to John is based on his identity as the pre-existent Word. But John's interrogators do not know the identity of the one who is standing among them. Contrast Mk 1:7, where the stronger one "is coming" rather than "is standing." Such a change is typical of John's focus on the presence of revelation and salvation in Jesus.

It is also typical of the Fourth Gospel that the Jews who oppose Jesus fail to recognize his identity. We will learn that failure to know Jesus is more than intellectual ignorance; it is a religious category derived from the Old Testament expressions about "knowing God" and it implies willful rejection of Jesus' revelation.

The Baptist's Witness to Jesus

The next double scene (vv. 29–34) has the Baptist testify to Jesus' identity. The change of day separates him from the interrogators of the previous scene, but no new audience has been provided for this scene. This "fading out" of the audience, to leave the speaker addressing the reader in isolation, is typical of Johannine style. With the abundant use of symbols, this technique enhances the timeless character of Johannine discourse. The twofold structure of this story forms a neat *inclusio:*

29–31	*32–34*
saw Jesus coming	saw Spirit coming
this is lamb of God	
takes away sin of the world	
(the one who comes after)	
did not know him	did not know him
baptize that he may be revealed	one who sent me to baptize
	reveals his identity
	he baptizes with Spirit
	is God's chosen one

The whole section contains parallels to synoptic stories about the baptism of Jesus. John the Baptist sees the Spirit descend on Jesus; Jesus will baptize with the Spirit; the Baptist announces that Jesus is the chosen one. But the Evangelist does not indicate that Jesus was ever baptized. He focuses throughout on the solemn pronouncements about Jesus' identity and mission.

The first section opens with the proclamation that Jesus is "lamb of God." This image seems to be an early Christian combination of two Old Testament images. Christians compared the death of Jesus to that of the Passover lamb (e.g., 1 Pt 1:19, Rv 5:6). The liturgical formula quoted in 1 Cor 5:17 shows that the comparison of Jesus and the lamb was much older than John. Allusions to this image are also found in the Johannine passion narrative (19:14, 36). The lamb image has been combined with that of the suffering servant, who bears the sins of the world (Is 53:7). Isaiah 53 was used by early Christians to describe Jesus as the servant (cf. Ac to 8:32, Mt 8:17, Heb 8:28). Thus the first thing that the reader learns about Jesus is that his mission will involve suffering and death.

In the second section, the descent of the Spirit designates Jesus as the chosen one. Jews thought that the Spirit of God would come upon the Messiah (T. Lev 18:7, T. Jud 24:1-3). Isaiah 52:1 says that the Spirit rested on the servant. Here the Evangelist says that the Spirit "remains" on Jesus. This expression could be a reflection of the servant language. The verb "to remain" is a Johannine favorite. When it is not used with its secular meaning, "to stay," the verb denotes the true relationship between Jesus (or his word or love) and the believer. The Evangelist here contrasts Jesus' possession of the Spirit with that of any other "spirit inspired" person. Not only is Jesus' possession of the Spirit unique, it is permanent. Therefore he is able to dispense the Spirit in the Spirit-filled baptism of the new age.

There is some difference in the manuscripts over the title the Baptist gives Jesus in verse 34. The earliest and the majority of manuscripts read "Son of God," but some have "Chosen One," an expression that does not occur elsewhere in John (Lk 23:35 is the only other example of it as a title for Jesus in the NT). Nevertheless, many commentators—followed by the NAB—feel that the latter expression was the original one. It is used of the servant in Is 42:1 and could be parallel to the expression "beloved" in the synoptics. Later copyists might have changed such an unusual expression to the more common "Son of God." Both expressions designate Jesus as the expected Messiah. John 1:49 shows that he knows the Jewish tradition, which used the expression "Son of God" to designate the messianic king.

John Sends Disciples

John's testimony to Jesus as the Lamb of God is repeated on the following day. It will provide Jesus with his first disciples. Throughout his gospel, the Evangelist presents us with a picture of faith as a response to testimony about Jesus. The expression "to follow Jesus" implies that a person has come to believe in him (e.g., 8:12, 10:27, 12:36). Later in the gospel, many people will refuse to believe in Jesus, even though they are given more elaborate testimony in word and sign than the simple declaration given by the Baptist (e.g., 5:31-40). Here, the Baptist's disciples provide a model for all later believers. When they hear the Baptist's testimony about Jesus, they immediately follow him. Throughout the gospel—even to the post-resurrection story about Thomas—belief on the basis of other people's testimony is followed by Jesus' personal call and an individual's response. The Baptist's disciples must respond to Jesus' call. This pattern in Johannine storytelling suggests that belief in Jesus proceeds in stages. First, a person responds to the testimony given by others; then, when he or she sees where Jesus dwells—in the community of believers after Jesus' death—he or she no longer bases faith on the testimony of others but on his or her experience of responding to Jesus.

Those of us who have been Christians since childhood may go through a similar development unreflectingly. Or we may suppose that faith is always based on the testimony or authority of others. We may then find outselves at a loss when we are challenged by others to give out own testimony about Jesus.

In John, the sequence of conversion is not complete until the new disciple becomes a witness for Jesus. Unlike the story in the other gospels, the calls of Andrew and Peter have been made a diptych. Andrew completes his conversion by first demonstrating his belief in calling Jesus "Messiah" and then by bringing another person, Simon, to Jesus. John connects the confession that Jesus is the Messiah (equals Christ) with Peter and the latter's change of name (cp. Mt 16:18). In this story, Jesus' personal call to Peter consists in his giving Simon a nickname—neither Cephas nor Peter was a proper name.

Galilean Disciples

Another change of days marks the next scene (vv. 43–51). The location has shifted from the area around Jerusalem to Galilee. Throughout the gospel we find alterations of scene between the two places. Some of these shifts are so impossible geographically that some commentators suggest that a later editor shifted the order of some chapters. But this alteration is so pervasive that we treat it as a compositional technique used by the Evangelist rather than as the creation of a later editor.

This section focuses on the second call—that of Nathanael. Jesus calls Philip directly (cp. Mk 2:14). Philip responds as a true disciple and goes to tell another that Jesus is the one predicted by Moses and the prophets. If Philip's phrase was intended to imply that Jesus is the prophet, like Moses and Elijah, he has now received all the titles refused by the Baptist. Nathanael's first reaction is skeptical. Such a reaction will be typical of Jews later in the gospel, particularly because Jesus' origins do not correspond to Old Testament predictions (cf. 6:42, 7:44, 9:29-41). But Nathanael does not allow his skepticism to keep him from coming to Jesus, who greets him as a true Israelite—much as he had greeted Peter by giving him a new name.

The cryptic dialogue between Jesus and Nathanael is typical of Johannine style. The meaning of Jesus' remark about seeing Nathanael under a fig tree is unclear. (Interpreters point to rabbinic references to studying the Torah under a fig tree.) Nathanael responds by declaring Jesus the Son of God, the expected messianic king. However, that declaration is not the high point of the dialogue. We see later in John that the traditional equation of Son of God with messianic king fails on both sides of the equation. Jesus' opponents do not understand his claim to be Son of God; nor do they understand the true nature of his kingship. The Evangelist constantly reminds us that Jesus fulfills such traditional expectations by transcending them, by asking us to re-evaluate the terms in which we understand the expected salvation.

John makes that change evident when Jesus promises Nathanael that he will see greater things than those to which he has just alluded. He explains the expression "greater things" by a saying about the coming of the Son of Man. The use of the double "amen," which the NAB translates "solemnly," is unique to John. The plural verb in "you will see" shows that the Evangelist is quoting an independent saying. It seems to be a development of the type of saying about the coming Son of Man that we find in Mk 14:62. The angels who accompany the Son of Man have been identified with those of Jacob's vision in Gn 28:12. The Evangelist is using this saying as a climax to both the dialogue and the entire collection of messianic titles which was used in the second half of the chapter. Compare the reference here to "seeing the Son of Man" with the reference to "seeing God" in verse 18. According to the Evangelist, both expectations can only be fulfilled in Jesus.

Further, he does not suppose that seeing God in/through Jesus will only occur in the future, at the end of the world— whereas, for example, the Son-of-Man saying in Mk 14:62 suggests that we will see Jesus as glorious Son of Man only at the judgment. No, for the Fourth Evangelist the glory of the Son of Man is to be manifest in the activity of Jesus on earth. Having clearly introduced him as the revelation of divine glory, the gospel now begins to describe his ministry.

2. Jesus Manifests His Glory in Signs

In the first chapter, the testimony of others brought Jesus his first disciples. Now he will perform "signs" in Galilee and Judea, which help those disciples believe in him. John has used traditional stories for the two main incidents in this chapter: the wedding at Cana and the cleansing of the temple; but he has retold these stories in a way that stresses two important theological themes: (1) the relationship between signs and faith in Jesus and (2) the crucifixion as the true revelation of Jesus' glory. John ties the first incident to the crucifixion by mentioning Jesus' "hour" and the presence of his mother, who will not appear again until the crucifixion. The traditional saying about the destruction of the temple links the second incident to the resurrection.

Many commentators have observed that John seems to attach symbolic significance to Galilee and Judea. Hostility to Jesus and his ministry consistently occurs in the latter. In this chapter, for example, the "sign" in Galilee leads the disiciples to believe; the "sign" in Jerusalem only causes people to ask for more signs. The Evangelist has probably taken over a contrast that existed in the "Jesus tradition" before him. It fits into the whole complex of binary symbols that he presents throughout the gospel. After the resurrection, the seemingly unsuccessful sign in Judea will bring the disciples to faith in Jesus' word.

John 2:1–12 *Wedding Feast at Cana*

John's account of the public ministry of Jesus includes seven miracles. All the others have some similarity to stories in the synoptic gospels but are not close enough to have been taken from them. Scholars suppose that John had a separate collection of the miracles of Jesus; but he has retold all the stories in his own idiom. It is possible to point out peculiarly Johannine expressions, theological motifs, and parenthetical comments which show how he understood the story. Most commentators agree that the following expressions have been added by the Evangelist: (1) "on the third day" (v. 1); (2) verse 4; (3) "for the purification of the Jews" (v. 6); (4) "and he did not know . . . had drawn water knew" (v. 9); (5) "in Cana of Galilee" (?), "he manifested his glory" (v. 11).

Compared with ancient and even modern counterparts, the story itself pays very little attention to the miraculous event. When he tells a miracle story, the Evangelist frequently omits any concluding demonstration of the success of the miracle or reaction by the crowd. Here, the identity of the miracleworker never becomes public.

Symbolism of the Story

Since this story is unlike any of the other miracles attributed to Jeses, some interpreters have suggested that it represents a Gentile-Christian attempt to portray Christ as a new Dionysus by associating him with a wine miracle. Certainly, Gentile converts may have understood the miracle in that context, but the Evangelist's addition in verse 6 shows that he understands it in the context of Jewish customs and feasts. Here, "empty" (the jars had no water in them) purification rituals are replaced by a vast (ca. 120 gal.) amount of wine. The Old Testament pictures the messianic age as a great banquet (e.g., Is 54:4–8; cp. Mt 22:1–4). Abundant wine is also frequently used as a symbol for the new age (Am 8:13, Hos 2:24, Jl 4:18, Is 29:17, Jer 31:5). In this story, then, the abundance of wine and its superior quality suggests that Jesus has brought the blessings of that age.

Since the Christian Eucharist is also portrayed as a fore-taste of the messianic banquet (e.g., Mk 14:25), some see a reference to the Eucharist here. However, the Evangelist has tied this miracle with purification rituals rather than with Passover and manna in the desert—common Old Testament analogues for the Eucharist. He uses both of these when he comes to the Eucharist in chapter 6. Therefore, this passage was probably not intended as a reference to the Eucharist.

The miracle, then, introduces Jesus as the one who fulfills the hopes for the new age. Other additions to the story are used by the Evangelist to tie it to larger concerns of the gospel. Jesus' answer to his mother in verse 4 introduces a very important perspective: Jesus' death is the hour of his glorification. His initial response to his mother's request is very harsh. The expression "What have you to do with me?" ("What has this concern of yours to do with me?" [NAB], is one interpretation of this awkward expression) could be used when one person objects to an injury unjustly received from another or when a person does not wish to become involved in something. The apparent refusal to comply with the request emphasizes Jesus' initiative in performing the miracle (cp. Jn 4:47-50, 11:22). The reader who is familiar with the language of the gospel realizes the significance of the reason Jesus gives. "Hour" refers to Jesus' crucifixion, which the Evangelist portrays as the time of his exaltation and return to the Father. Verse 9 also uses language that has important overtones to one familiar with the entire gospel. The waiter is said to taste the wine "without knowing where it had come from." Later, we find that Jesus' opponents think they know where *he* has come from but, in fact, are ignorant of his divine origin (cf. 7:27ff.).

The consistent use of language which has symbolic significance within the context of the gospel as a whole suggests that the gospel was not intended to convert people to Christianity or to be understood at a single reading. It is a work for the believer, to be studied. Much of its symbolic language may have been used in the liturgy and preaching of John's community.

Since "glory" is also an important term in John, many presume that the Evangelist added verse 11. Others point out that miracle stories were supposed to manifest the power of the wonderworker. They suggest that the author has substituted the word "glory" for "power" but has taken the verse from his source. The Evangelist, as we shall see, does not have a simple evaluation of miraculous events. He shows that miracles lead as much to confusion and disbelief as to faith. Jesus' glory is really seen only in the crucifixion.

Taken on the literal level, this story would seem to be a fantastic magic trick. Even today we hear about people who claim to have miraculous powers of healing or performing other feats through "mind control." Just as in Jesus' day, people often respond to such a person with curiosity, attempt to get him or her to perform more miracles, and debate the source or value of such powers. But John refuses to engage in this kind of literal-minded debate over Jesus' powers. He tells the story in such a way as to remind his readers that what counts is the symbolism, not the deed. We learn that Jesus has "brought" the promised time of salvation, that he comes from the Father, and that he will truly show his glory at the hour of his crucifixion.

Verse 12 is a brief transitional verse. Many of the transitions between scenes in John are equally awkward. Mark

3:31ff. tells a story of an encounter between Jesus and his family which concludes with the declaration that those who do the will of the Father are his true family. Perhaps the Evangelist wishes to remind his readers of a similar story that is known to them. Others think that this verse was part of the source from which John derived the Cana miracle.

Signs and Glory in the Fourth Gospel

The Fourth Gospel usually refers to the miracles of Jesus as "signs." In the synoptic tradition, "sign" frequently means an indication that the end is at hand. Though the wine symbolism of the Cana story clearly has eschatological overtones, the designation "sign" may also apply to the necessity of seeing beyond the literal event to its symbolic significance. Clearly, John can use the word "sign" in an apocalyptic sense when he is quoting traditional sayings that reject seeking for signs (4:48, 6:26). The gospel shows people responding to miracles in a variety of ways:

1 Some see the signs and do not believe at all (3:19–20, 9:41, 11:47).

2 Others respond to Jesus as a great wonderworker. This response is rejected (2:23–25, 3:2–3, 4:45–48, 7:5).

3 The believer is able to see the miracle as a sign of Jesus' glory (2:11, 4:53, 6:69, 9:38, 11:40).

Since John ties the glory of Jesus to the crucifixion, he is not supposing that the miracles would prove the glory of Jesus to a nonbeliever. He is not talking about the kind of earthly fame achieved by wonderworkers who appear on later-night talk shows. When John refers to Jesus' glory, he draws upon the OT language about the glory of God, which is associated with the deeds by which God delivers his people and with his presence among them. Jesus' ministry will perform both functions. The Father is present or visible in Jesus (1:46, 14:9). The crucifixion is the saving manifestation of his glory (12:23, 28, 17:1-5).

The Signs' Source

Despite the fact that the Evangelist presents a nuanced view of the type of response appropriate to miracles, the stories themselves seem to presuppose a simpler connection between miracles and faith. They treat the miracles as the beginning of faith. For example, although 4:48 has criticized faith based on signs, 4:53 suggests that the healing led the official and his household to become Christians. Other ambiguities in the narratives suggest that the Evangelist has used an older miracle collection, which may have been used for missionary purposes. The miracles were thought to prove that Jesus was indeed the Messiah or Savior—much as some groups still use miracles to prove the value of faith. We frequently find the simpler views of the Evangelist's sources in the gospel alongside his more nuanced theology.

Several attempts have been made to spell out the contents of John's miracle source, which scholars call the "signs' source"; but detailed verbatim reconstructions are highly speculative. Sometimes a theological vocabulary that is peculiar to John, as well as his literary style, make it clear that the Evangelist has made additions to the story. In other cases, comparison with miracle stories in the synoptics provides suggestions for the scope of the story John is using. The following stories seem to be derived from that source.

A. Stories in Galilee, location Cana
    1. Wedding feast (2:1-3, 5-11)
    2. Royal official's son (4:4-54)

B. Galilee, Sea of Tiberias
   3. Feeding 5,000 (6:1–3, 5, 7–14)
   4. Walking on water (6:15b–22)
   5. Catch of fish (21:1–3, 5–11)
C. Jerusalem and vicinity
   6. Healing the paralytic (5:2f., 5–9, 13f.?)
   7. Healing the blind man (9:1–3a, 6f.)
   8. Raising Lazarus (11:1–3, 7, 11, 17–19, 23–34,
      35f., 41, 43–45)

The stories in the source may have contained brief geo-graphical introductions, such as 4:46. Many scholars think that Jn 20:30–31a was originally the conclusion to that source, since it suggests a direct connection between the miracles and belief in Jesus as Son of God.

Although the Evangelist preserves such positive remarks about the miracles, he never portrays them as a direct source of faith. When Jesus speaks positively of his ministry, he refers to his work or works (note the shift in 6:26–29), which he does as the will of the Father. This term embraces all the activity of Jesus, miracles and teaching alike (e.g., 14:10, 17:4). Some commentators suggest that when "work" is applied to miracles the Evangelist means to include the discourses with which he follows most of them. Jesus' works, not his signs, are part of the testimony he invokes in his controversies with the authorities.

We may find John's caveats about faith based on the miraculous helpful in dealing with out own "wonderworkers" who attract public attention. The Evangelist does not deny that Jesus worked miracles or that some people found them a source of faith, but he sees the natural human tendency to seek miracles for their own sake as leading people away from the truth about Jesus. He is very clear that the salva-tion brought by Jesus is not one of earthly peace or an easy solution to life's problems. We live in a time in which people flock after a variety of "instant" therapies and fads. John's approach to miracles warns us that such shallow belief in instant remedies is more likely to obscure truth and salvation than to reveal it.

John 2:13-25 *Cleansing the Temple*

Unlike the synoptics, where Jesus' ministry lasts a year and culminates in Jerusalem, John has him journeying back and forth between Galilee and Jerusalem. This Passover is the first of three mentioned in the gospel (2:13, 6:4, 11:55). Some interpreters feel that a longer ministry is more probable. Mark 11:15-28 parr. separate the action in the temple from the challenge to Jesus' authority. John may be more original in connecting the two, as recent studies of Markan technique have shown that he likes to interlock episodes from different stories. But the chronological question still remains: Did Jesus act against the temple early in his career or did that action precipitate his arrest, as the synoptics suggest?

Most commentators think the synoptics more original. All versions of the story suggest that Jesus had a large following in Jerusalem, which would fit in better with the end of his ministry. An attack against the temple at the busiest festival, when Jewish and Roman authorities were on alert to prevent trouble, would be exactly the sort of thing to provoke action by the authorities, as the synoptics suggest. Thus we must suppose that John has relocated the scene toward the beginning of the ministry. It provides an explanation for the hostility that Jesus will consistently experience from the authorities ("the Jews" [v. 19]) in Jerusalem.

Jesus' symbolic action and criticism of corruption in the temple is reminiscent of the OT prophets (e.g., Jer 7:11, Zech 14:21, Is 55:7). In the context of this chapter, this criticism continues the criticism implied in the first incident, where the empty purification jars were filled with wine. The cleansing and purification of the temple was often associated with the new age. Prophetic criticism of the temple was not directed at institutionalized religion as such, but the prophets saw people assuming that their religious obligations were limited to the specifically religious ceremonies and neglecting their duties toward the poor and suffering. Sometimes the religious leadership was criticized for fostering this illusion. (We are aware of similar tendencies in our own society.) Purification of the temple, then, stood for the hope that the whole people would come to worship God as he intended. At the same time, for many the temple was a powerful symbol of God's presence with his people. Every adult Jew, no matter where he lived, contributed to its upkeep.

Jewish sources provide other examples of individuals who predicted the destruction of the temple. About A.D. 30, according to rabbinic sources (T. B., Giffin, 56a; Mid Rab Lam I.5.31), R. Zadok began fasting to forestall the temple's destruction. The Jewish historian, Josephus (*War*, VI, v. 3), reports that a certain Jesus ben Annaniah went around Jerusalem predicting the destruction of the temple in A.D. 62. He was persecuted for his preaching.

The Quotations

This story contains two allusions to the OT. First, Jesus' saying in verse 16 recalls Zec 14:26. The synoptic versions of this story have a combination of Is 55:7 and Jer 7:11

at this point. That difference is one example of the divergences between the Johannine and the synoptic traditions, which persuades scholars that John's tradition about Jesus was independent of the synoptics.

The Evangelist interrupts the story with another OT quotation from Ps 69, which is frequently quoted in the NT. Verse 22 shows that "recall" is a term John uses for the process by which Christians came to understand the life of Jesus better after his resurrection. Often they did this by finding passages in the OT to show that God predicted in advance what had happened to Jesus. Since Ps 69 was such an important part of the process, the Evangelist may have expected his readers to recall the context of the passage he quotes:

> I have become an outcast to my brothers,
> a stranger to my mother's sons,
> Because zeal for your house consumes me,
> and the insults of those who blaspheme you
> fall upon me [Ps 69:9f.]

The Evangelist has changed the tense of the verb from past to future, "will consume" (the NAB translation obscures this difference by translating both the psalm and John in the present. If the Evangelist and not his tradition is responsible for the change, he may wish to see this text as a prediction of the death of Jesus. The preceding verse may fit into the context of the Johannine narrative because we have just seen Jesus with his mother and brothers (v. 12). Later (7:1ff.), Jesus' "brothers" try to persuade him to go to Jerusalem, where his life is threatened. Thus, like the Cana story, this one also points forward to the death of Jesus.

Jesus Defends His Authority

The authorities immediately demand some proof of Jesus'
right to act as he has done. Such requests for a sign are
always examples of hostility and disbelief. Frequently, debates between Jesus and the authorities in the Fourth Gospel
reflect the situation of later Christians. Here Jesus' response
has been brought into line with its interpretation as a reference to his resurrection. The synoptic tradition (Mk 14:38
parr.) has Jesus speak of rebuilding the temple whereas John
has "raising up." But verses 21–22 make it clear that this
interpretation of Jesus' saying was reached only after his
resurrection. For Christians, Jesus' resurrection and exaltation
into heaven was the final proof of his authority. Verse 22
parallels that authority with Scripture itself—perhaps a reference to the OT quotation in verse 17. Controversy stories
later in the gospel will return to the question of Jesus' authority. The farewell discourses will make it clear that full
understanding of Jesus was possible only after the resurrection
and the coming of the Paraclete. Since Christians in the
Evangelist's day were a persecuted minority, they were perhaps even more conscious than many of us are that many
people would not accept the authority of Jesus.

Both stories in this chapter place the authority of Jesus
against Jewish religious institutions. In the first, the purification rituals have been replaced with the wine of the eschatological banquet. In this story, Jesus' authority is equal to
that of Scripture, and the temple has in effect been replaced
as the place of religious devotion. At the very beginning of
his ministry in John, Jesus comes into conflict with the
religious authorities. That conflict will intensify throughout
the story, until it culminates in the crucifixion. In John's
day, to be a Christian meant to choose between the authority

of Jesus as the revelation of God and the traditional religious authorities of Judaism, who claimed the backing of Moses and Scripture.

Jesus Knows All

The reader of the Fourth Gospel is never allowed to take faith for granted. The opening stories of the gospel showed how the disciples came to faith in Jesus. John 2:22 concluded that process by pointing out the importance of their post-resurrection understanding of Jesus in making it possible for them to formulate the picture of his authority and significance. But we are now presented with the other side of the coin. Not everyone who is first attracted to Jesus will go on to become a believer. Some people based their faith on signs that they saw Jesus do, but such faith is not accepted. Later (5:42), Jesus says to his opponents that he knows they do not have the love of God in them. Thus when the Evangelist speaks of Jesus' knowing what is in a person (an expression used of God in the OT), he is referring to Jesus' knowledge of that person's religious disposition. He is not presenting Jesus as some trick mind-reader. The next chapter opens with a dialogue between Jesus and someone who "comes" to Jesus because of the signs Jesus has done. But even though he has seen those signs, he will be unable to understand Jesus' message of salvation.

The allusions and symbols in this chapter have made it possible for the Evangelist to continue his presentation of Jesus as the one who has fulfilled all the OT promises for the messianic age. At the same time, he makes it clear that this will only be complete with the death and resurrection of Jesus. His teaching and ministry cannot be understood without the climax to which they led. He also begins to introduce the varieties of response elicited by Jesus' ministry. Not even all of those who call themselves believers may be trusted until the basis of their faith is known. Scenes of hostility and rejection become more frequent as the gospel proceeds. Some authors have pointed out that John is more consistently oriented toward the crucifixion than the other gospels.

Those who feel that John's picture of Jesus loses sight of his humanity should remember that the Evangelist never allows us to forget that Jesus' ministry is leading to his death. Further, the Evangelist makes it clear that the picture of Jesus he presents derives from the faith in Jesus that the disciples reached after his resurrection. Even believers did not grasp the full significance of Jesus during his lifetime.

3. Birth from Above

The previous chapter ended by pointing out that a faith based solely on Jesus' signs was insufficient; this one begins with a dialogue between Jesus and Nicodemus, who comes to Jesus precisely because he has seen such signs. When Jesus initially refused to work his first miracle because it was not yet his hour (2:4), the reader was warned that Jesus' true significance could only be understood from the perspective of his crucifixion. This chapter will explain that salvation is tied to belief in Jesus as the crucified and exalted one.

Literary Problems

Chapter 3 poses several literary problems for the interpreter. These problems are typical of the difficulties Johannine narrative presents.

First, the narrative seems to drop or change speakers without warning. Does the scene with Nicodemus end at verse 12 or at verse 15? The literary parallel between this scene and the earlier one with Nathanael (1:49–51) suggests that verse 15 is the conclusion:

1:49–51	*3:9–15*
Jesus' cryptic statement leads Nathanael to confess that he is Son of God (v. 49)	Nicodemus cannot understand Jesus' cryptic statement (v. 9)
Jesus' question: you believe on the basis of the fig tree (v. 50a)	Jesus' question: are you a teacher and do not know? (v. 10)

You will see greater things (v. 50b)	If you do not believe earthly things, how heavenly ones? (vv. 11f.)
Heavens open and angels go up and down on the Son of Man (v. 51)	No one has gone up to heaven except the Son of Man who has come down (v. 13)
	Son of Man to be lifted up so that believers have eternal life (14f.)

The Nicodemus dialogue is similar to the Nathanael dialogue, except that Nicodemus is cast in the role of one who does not understand Jesus, rather than in the role of believer. The promise of salvation is made to those who believe the heavenly things that Nicodemus cannot grasp: the uniqueness of Jesus as revealer and the necessity of his death for salvation.

The discourse material in verses 16-21 and 31-36 poses a second, problem. Verses 31-36 follow a speech by John the Baptist but do not seem to be spoken by him. The speaker is more appropriately either Jesus or the Evangelist himself. Some interpreters suggest that vv. 31-36 should follow—or even precede—vv. 16-21, since they pick up the from above/from below contrast of the Nicodemus scene. They point out that such an arrangement would bring the two sections on John the Baptist together (3:22ff, 4:1ff.). Other instances of such "free floating" discourse material in the gospel are equally difficult to assess; there is no manuscript evidence for such rearrangements. Other interpreters suggest that these loose fragments were added later by the Evangelist or a disciple. Since we deal with the text as it stands, it seems simplest to understand vv. 31-36 as a summary of the chapter composed by the Evangelist. The following pattern then dominates the narrative from 3:1 to 4:3: dialogue—discourse—

John the Baptist—discourse—John the Baptist. A new dialogue begins at 4:4.

Johannine Discourse

A major problem of Johannine interpretation is assessing
the function and intent of Johannine discourse material. On
one extreme, excessively dogma-oriented interpreters seek
support in it for the trinitarian and Christological formula-
tions of later centuries. On the other extreme—influenced
by the great commentary of Rudolf Bultmann—some argue
that the discourse material in John is essentially contentless;
that statements such as those made here have no cognitive
reference; that they are not intended to convey information.
Rather, they are performative. They demand acceptance of
Jesus as revealer and Savior but do not convey information
about the content of that revelation or the nature of salvation. Difficulties in interpreting Johannine discourse material
arise, in part, from the Western bifurcation of human beings
into intellect and will, in part from a lack of sensitivity to
symbolic religious discourse, and in part from the inevitable
loss of the experiential context to which the gospel was
addressed.

We should remember that the author is often using well-
established religious symbols and language in unexpected
contexts and relationships. Minimally, the revelation may
be said to have content in terms of these symbols. Sometimes John's symbolic language serves a universalizing function. Such general symbols permit people from a wide
variety of cultural contexts to appropriate the Christian
revelation by seeing Christ as the fulfillment of all humanity's
religious aspirations. But the way in which John reuses OT
and earlier Christian religious language suggests that he has
an even more specific intent: to provide a new understanding

of the traditional religious language. Where John responds to charges raised by Jewish opponents of Christianity, the discourse material is even more directly cognitive. The reader learns how to answer the charges against Christianity by hearing how Jesus answered similar charges.

At the same time, John is explicitly interested in changing the attitudes and behavior of his audience. He is writing for believers (20:30f.), not for disinterested historians. Insofar as the religious symbols he used already carried affective and performative significance for his audience, his rearrangement of them cannot help but influence, change, or reshape the experience of the believer.

Although he wishes to affect the behavior of his readers, the Evangelist's metaphors cannot simply be interpreted as demands that we "make a decision" for Christ. In fact, in a religious context, decision language is highly ambiguous. We tend to associate circumstances with it that are under our own control. Yet faith in the Fourth Gospel can hardly be associated with the exercise of will that is usually connoted by "decide." Use of such language about the Spirit in this chapter shows that, in some respects, the believer's faith is not his or her own creation, any more than the content of his or her religious knowledge is his/her own intellectual discovery. At the same time, those who do not heed the revelation are considered culpable. They are not excused on the basis of some natural inability to respond positively. John will use a variety of metaphors to explain the difference between believer and nonbeliever, but they do not seem to constitute a systematic, theological account of disbelief.

John 3:1-15 *Dialogue with Nicodemus*

This dialogue uses a typical Johannine technique: ironic

double meaning. Jesus' protagonist makes a statement which is true, understood from the perspective of Johannine symbolism, but which is not true as the speaker understands it. Jesus replies on the symbolic level with a statement that seems to be beside the point. Misunderstanding results from the fact that the two are speaking on different levels. Some interpreters suggest that the reader's sense of being "in on the joke" makes him or her feel superior to Nicodemus. If the Fourth Gospel originated in a community that was involved in debate with the Jews, it would hardly be an accident that a "teacher of Israel" is unable to understand truths that are known to every Christian.

Nicodemus is an ambiguous figure. The fact that he comes at night puts him in a negative light. He cannot understand. Others suggest that his association with the burial of Jesus dicates that the Evangelist considers him a secret believer. When Nicodemus defends Jesus (7:50ff.), he suffers a put-down similar to the one he receives in this passage: he does not understand the Old Testament. It seems, then, that John never accepts or rejects Nicodemus. He is a positively motivated individual who is caught in the middle—neither quite teacher of Israel nor Christian believer. His portrayal somewhat ameliorates the rigid dualism suggested by much Johannine symbolism; that is, not all nonbelievers are hostile enemies. At the same time, John does not hold that a non-Christian can be saved, as the dialogue makes clear. Nicodemus may also represent religious leaders who are hesitant to believe (cf. 12:42).

Birth from Above

From seeing Jesus' signs, Nicodemus comes to accept Jesus as a teacher on the same level with himself (vv. 1–3). He uses the expression "from God" to indicate Jesus' authority, without realizing the unique sense in which Jesus is "from God." Jesus' answer begins to expound that Johannine sense by referring to the necessity that the believer be born "from above."

Verses 3 and 5 are the only places in John where the expression "kingdom of God," so common in the synoptics, occurs. Verse 5 has the more traditional expression "enter" the kingdom, while verse 3 speaks of "seeing" the kingdom. It is difficult to say whether that difference represents variants within the tradition as it came to the Evangelist or whether verse 3 represents his modification of the tradition to accommodate a realized eschatology. The kingdom may be "seen" by the believer without implying a cosmic destruction of this world.

Nicodemus takes the Greek word *anothen* to mean "again," rather than "above." He challenges Jesus to debate by taking the most ridiculous interpretation of his statement (v. 4). This procedure is typical in such debates and does not imply that Nicodemus is incredibly stupid. But Jesus does not accept the challenge to engage in the type of debate that might be expected between two teachers of the law. Instead, he repeats the earlier assertion but substitutes "water and the Spirit" for "from above."

Jews expected a new outpouring of the Spirit at the end of the age. Sometimes the Spirit is symbolized by water (e.g., Is 44:3, Jub 1:23–25, I QS 4:19–21). Post-exilic Judaism could also speak of pious individuals as "sons of God" (Wis 5:5, Ps Sol 17:30, Sir 4:10, 23:1, 4). The peculiarity of John's metaphor lies in the combination of "beget" and the outpouring of the Spirit that establishes that Sonship. This twist is typical of John's use of traditional symbolism. The metaphor of begetting may be derived from Ps 2:7: "You are my son. Today I have begotten you." This text was used frequently of Jesus in the NT and occurs in connection with his baptism (Mt 3:17 par.). John may have then applied the language of begetting to Christian baptism (cf. Jn 1:12).

Verses 6–8 expand Jesus' assertion. The contrast between flesh and spirit is not a body/soul contrast but a contrast between natural human birth and that given from above by the Spirit. Because this use of spirit/flesh is similar to early creedal statements about Jesus (Rm 1:3f., 1 Tm 3:16), some have taken verses 3, 5, and 8 as references to Jesus. It seems to us, however, that the language of these verses stems from the baptismal tradition of the Johannine community, which had been modeled on traditions about the baptism of Jesus.

Verse 8 uses a proverbial saying about wind (cf. Eccl 11:5) to draw an analogy between wind and spirit. Without examples of the use of the proverb, the exact force of the analogy is difficult to determine. Dodd (*Tradition,* pp. 364f.) compares this passage with the parable of the seed growing secretly (Mk 4:26–29), while Schnackenburg (1:374) suggests that it emphasizes the mysteriousness of divine grace.

Nicodemus has not understood any of this teaching about baptism (vv. 9f.). Jesus points this out to him almost sarcastically. Nicodemus has nothing further to say.

Jesus' Authority as Teacher

Having silenced the Jewish teacher, Jesus contrasts his own authority with that of Nicodemus (v. 11). His "we know" picks up that of Nicodemus in verse 2. The plural "we" contrasts the Christians as a group against the Jews as represented by Nicodemus. Jesus' rhetorical question to

Nicodemus employs a well-known cliché: If you cannot understand earthly (i.e., elementary) things, how do you expect to understand heavenly ones? Or, as we might say: If you cannot even do algebra, how to you expect to be another Einstein? Similar expressions were used in antiquity to rebuke slow or obtuse students. The "earthly" things in the contrast may refer to the OT or to language and beliefs derived from Judaism, such as the outpouring of God's Spirit in the new age. Just as he did in 1:48–51, Jesus follows an "earthly" thing with an exposition of a heavenly one.

Jesus' claim to authority is based on his heavenly origin (v. 13). The denial that anyone has gone up into heaven except the Son of Man is probably aimed at other claims to heavenly revelation. The OT wisdom tradition insists that man cannot know what is in the heavens (Wis 9:16–18, Prv 30:3f., 2 Bar 3:29). But in John's day a variety of apocalyptic revelations claimed to report the things that had been seen by ancient seers on their heavenly journeys. The past tense, "has gone up," could refer to such seers: Adam, Enoch, Ezra, and even Moses himself. From the Evangelist's perspective, it also represents the fact that Jesus has gone up into heaven and is there with his Father.

The "Son of Man" imagery in John has several peculiarities which suggest that earlier Christian language has been reinterpreted. The apocalyptic associations of the term are still evident in the reference to going into heaven. In Dn 7:13ff., the Son of Man ascends to the heavenly throne, but here he is characterized as the one who has first come from heaven. Earlier Christian tradition has the Son of Man (= Jesus) come down from heaven at the judgment (Mk 13:26, 14:62, Rv 1:7). "Son of Man could also be used as a self-designation by the earthly Jesus, but the two traditions were not connected. Here the Evangelist has understood

Jesus' heavenly origin to mean that the earthly Jesus was the Son of Man come from heaven.

The Crucifixion/Exaltation

The "heavenly things" that Nicodemus could not understand turn out to be Jesus' crucifixion and exaltation into heaven. The passion prediction is the third type of Son-of-Man saying in the Jesus tradition (cf. Mk 8:31 par.). John brings all three of these images together: Jesus is/has come as heavenly Son of Man, he suffers as such, and is exalted into heaven. John 3:14f. is the only place in the NT which uses the typology from Nm 21:28ff. to explain the saving effect of the crucifixion. Perhaps the Evangelist created the typology himself by looking in the OT for metaphors of exaltation.

John always portrays the crucifixion as the moment of Jesus' exaltation. Thus his theology of the cross contrasts with earlier views which had seen it as a humiliation only overcome by the exaltation of the ascension. John will never separate crucifixion/exaltation and will never use language about the crucifixion which would suggest that it was degrading. All three passion predictions stress the crucifixion as elevation (3:14, 8:28, 12:32). Jesus' death is his ascent or return to the Father (6:62, 13:1) or his glorification (12:23, 13:31).

Jewish tradition frequently associated resurrection with the vindication and exaltation of the righteous who had been humiliated and killed by the wicked. Since John never treats Jesus' death as humiliation, we are not surprised that the resurrection is mentioned only in explanatory comments by the Evangelist (2:19, 10:18) and does not form part of the passion predictions, as it does in the other gospels.

The Numbers tupology attributes a saving significance to the death of Jesus without using sacrificial language. Some commentators have been misled by the fact that John does not use sacrificial, victim/expiation, language about the crucifixion into thinking that the crucifixion had no saving significance in his theology. (John 1:29 shows that the Evangelist's tradition contained sacrificial language, even though he has not exploited it.) The wisdom tradition may have paved the way for John's view when it spoke of the serpent as the sign of salvation (Wis 16:6f.). The person who can see the crucified Jesus as the exalted Son of Man will have eternal life.

While sacrificial offerings were a common part of the religious life of ancient man—Jew and pagan alike—we, who are not accustomed to such practices, may find John's more direct approach easier to assimilate: God grants the believer eternal life. He is not "bought off" by the violent death of his Son, any more than Moses' raising up a sign for the people was an appeasement of God. God had already turned to save his people. But to receive that salvation they had to look upon the sign he established. What Nicodemus will not be able to understand is that the crucified Jesus is the definitive sign of God's salvation.

"Son of Man" in the Fourth Gospel

At several points in the narrative confession of Jesus as Son of Man is the culmination of all possible statements about his identity. Most of John's allusions to the symbol carry overtones of apocalyptic images derived from Dn 7, where the Son of Man comes or is enthroned in glory with the angels and acts as judge (cf. Mk 14:62). These sayings frequently occur in debates over the messianic identity of

Jesus and the proper interpretation of the OT promises. For example, 1:51 concludes a series of messianic titles with an enigmatic saying about the heavens opening and the angels ascending/descending upon the Son of Man. Open heavens, ascent/descent, and angelic hosts all belong to the picture of the Son of Man as judge that earlier Christian tradition had formed on the basis of Daniel. Yet the peculiar use of those images, made possible by the allusion to Gn 28, is not what one would expect of an author who is merely copying earlier tradition. Rather, the verse suggests that the vision of Jesus as Son of Man is divorced from the context of his judgment at the end of the world. (John 5:27b shows that the Evangelist knew the tradition about the Son of Man as judge.)

As in the synoptics, John uses the Son-of-Man symbol in three predictions of the passion (3:14, 8:28, 12:31, cp. Mk 8:31). But as 3:14 shows, he does not take an OT prophecy about suffering as the base for his predictions. Instead, he focuses on analogies with the "lifting up" of the crucifixion and thus connects it with the Danielic picture of the Son of Man ascending to a heavenly throne. John's use of "Son of Man" seems to be a re-evaluation of earlier Christian apocalyptic expectations. The earlier traditions have Jesus, the crucified, vindicated by his exaltation into heaven. When he returns in glory as Son of Man, he will triumph over his enemies. The glory of Jesus as Son of Man was usually associated with the second coming, though Luke can speak of the resurrection/ascension as Jesus' exaltation into heavenly glory (Lk 22:69, 24:36, Acts 7:55f.). In John, however, Jesus returns to glory he had before (17:5, 24). He does not assume a new position of glory. He speaks of the earthly Jesus as the Son of Man, who has descended from heaven, rather than associate that descent with Jesus' coming as judge.

John thus portrays the earthly Jesus as the salvation-bringing Son of Man. Debates about the messianic activity of Jesus, in comparison with what is said of the Messiah or Moses, culminate in sayings about the Son of Man (1:51, 6:27, 53, 9:29ff.). The controversy stories consistently assert that Jesus is superior to Moses. Belief in Jesus requires a person to take a different view of the OT and the activity of the Messiah than was common in John's day, and the Son-of-Man symbol capsulizes that new understanding. In Jn 12:31–34 the crowd understands Jesus' prediction of his crucifixion/exaltation as a reference to the lifting up of the Son of Man. But it rejects his claims on the basis of the widely held view that the Messiah was to remain forever. Jesus does not debate the crowds' interpretation of Scripture, but makes a solemn pronouncement that implies its ultimate condemnation. The apocalyptic Son-of-Man sayings in the synoptics are often associated with pronouncements that imply the condemnation of Jesus' opponents (cf. Mk 14:62). Although John sees judgment as a present reality, based on a person's response to Jesus, the judgment overtones of his Son-of-Man sayings remain. They are often found in contexts where Jesus faces opposition. For example, 6:62 is a judgment oracle against those who have been scandalized by Jesus' teaching on the Eucharist; 8:28 is against hostile Jews who do not recognize that Jesus is from the Father. Thus the Christian reader sees that those who reject Jesus stand condemned by God.

The frequency with which Jesus' opponents bring objections against his claims on the basis of Scripture or the common understanding about the Messiah shows that the Evangelist is well aware that Jesus' claims to be the Messiah cannot be immediately identified with what many Jews expected the Messiah to be. Those expectations and their scriptural foundations might even hinder a person from believing that Jesus is indeed Son of Man.

We are so accustomed to understand language about the Messiah and the Son of Man in terms defined by the life of Jesus that we often find it difficult to appreciate the problems presented by Jesus' preaching and that of the earliest Christians. We sometimes suppose that all problems for belief are posed by modern, secular culture; but Jesus presented difficulties for the accepted religious traditions of his day. The Evangelist meets such objections in a variety of ways. Sometimes—as in many of the debates over Scripture—he does not engage in an argument to disprove the opponents' reading of its text but insists that Jesus be allowed to define what it means to be Messiah. In other cases it is possible to recast earlier traditions in such a way as to meet an objection. The Son-of-Man image in the Fourth Gospel shows signs of such recasting, but the Evangelist also seems to use it at the culmination of controversies to indicate Jesus' independence of the way in which people are trying to categorize him.

John 3:16-21 *The Mission of the Son*

The narrative suddenly shifts to speaking of Jesus in the third person at verse 16. Some interpreters suggest that passages such as this one represent the Evangelist's own preaching or reflection.

Verse 16 is the only place in John where God is said to love the world. Most of the love language in the gospel occurs in the farewell discourses, where it describes the new relationship between the Father and Son and the believers. (The love language in 1 Jn is similar.) John speaks of the Father "giving" the Son. A compound form of the same verb, "hand over," was a technical term in early Christianity for Jesus' crucifixion (cf. Gal 2:20, Rom 8:32). Some commentators suggest that John avoids using the technical term because he wishes to stress the fact that Jesus is sent by the Father. The whole verse may reflect the liturgy of the Johannine community. The antithesis, perish/eternal life, occurs in 6:27 as the contrast between the OT manna and the Christian Eucharist; in 10:28 the shepherd gives his sheep eternal life so that they will not perish.

Jesus' Presence as Judgment

The verses which follow (16–18) make it clear that Jesus' presence brings judgment. They have a parallel in a later, isolated fragment which also uses the imagery of light to describe that judgment:

3:16–18		*12:46–48*	
16:	believer does not perish but has eternal life	46b:	that believers not remain in darkness
17:	God did not send the Son to judge but to save	47:	I have not come to judge but to save
18:	believer not judged; unbeliever already judged	48:	one who does not keep my words is judged; my word condemns him on the last day
19:	judgment is the coming of light; men prefer darkness	46:	I came as light into the world that believers might not remain in darkness

Study of the Son-of-Man passages has already shown that the Evangelist is not much interested in future, apocalyptic scenarios. The earthly Jesus came as Son of Man. These passages show that the Evangelist can even extend that metaphor to include the picture of Son of Man as judge. Jesus' presence in the world brings about the separation of believers and nonbelievers. People choose their own judgment. But the Evangelist continually stresses the fact that Jesus' mission was to save people, not to condemn them. The image of light conveys. a picture of that salvation as readily available to all. John does not use the image in such a way as to suggest that only a small amount of light is trapped in the darkness and only a few people can attain it. Rather, he supposes that everyone who comes into contact with the light has a genuine choice to accept or reject it. God's intent is salvation, not judgment.

If God has sent a true, saving revelation into the world with the intent of saving all and not just a select few, it is necessary to explain why not all have believed. Nicodemus seemed to be a type of person who could not quite accept the truth, even though he felt that Jesus might be a legitimate teacher. Verses 19b–21 explain nonbelief by suggesting that some people reject the revelation because they do not follow God's commandments. The expressions "to do wickedness" and "to do truth" are Semitic. The Dead Sea Scrolls use the. expression "to do truth" (e.g., I QS 1:5, 5:3, 8:12) to indicate that members of the sect carry out everything commanded by God. The verb, translated "be exposed" (NAB) in verse 20, has a range of meanings that is difficult to capture in English: expose, condemn, convict, reprimand. Thus "exposure" of the person's deeds implies that he or she will be condemned for them. Although the gospel itself, contains practically no formal ethical teaching, this passage shows that the Evangelist presupposes such teaching, since he can invoke differences in ethical performance to explain why some people do not believe.

This is not the only explanation for nonbelief advanced in the gospel. The fact that the Evangelist has several explanations is one indication that his dualistic language is not part of a rigid system that classifies people in one category or another. Whatever explanations he attempts, the Evangelist never compromises his conviction that Jesus is the only way to salvation.

John 3:22-30 *Jesus and John the Baptist*

This unit seems to have been an independent piece at one time, since its introduction does not fit the context. Jesus was already in Jerusalem, but here, he and his disciples are said to come into Judea. (The location has not been positively identified.) Some interpreters think that this passage belongs with the other Baptist materials in chapter 1, somewhere after 1:34, since verse 25 refers to the Baptist's previous testimony to Jesus. By moving this passage, the Evangelist was able to concentrate on the discipleship stories in the first chapter. Further, the allusions to baptism in the Nicodemus story make this chapter an appropriate setting for an incident with John the Baptist. This setting contrasts Christian baptism with the baptism practiced by John and his followers. Many commentators point to the traditions in Acts, which imply that disciples of the Baptist continued to baptize after their master's death and came into some contact with Christian missionaries (cf. Acts 10:37, 13:24, 18:25, 19:3). They suggest that John was aware of a similar situation and so has stressed the view that all of John the Baptist's activity was testimony to Jesus—that he did not intend to found a sect of his own.

Verse 24 seems to be a parenthetical addition, based on

the tradition—preserved in the synoptics—that Jesus did not begin his ministry until after John's death.

The testimony of the Baptist (vv. 27–30) fits into the pattern established in the first chapter. His function is to testify that Jesus is the Messiah and that Jesus' ministry and its success are willed by God (v. 27). Verse 28 refers directly back to 1:20.

The Baptist's image of himself as best man and Jesus as bridegroom does not have any parallels in the OT, where God is the bridegroom of Israel. But Christians compared Jesus to the bridegroom (cf. Mk 2:19ff.) and probably formulated this image. The Baptist's final words to his disciples carry the same message as his earlier testimony: he is subordinate to Jesus; Jesus is the only one whom any disciple of the Baptist should follow.

John 3:31–36 *Summary*

This section repeats themes that belong to the earlier parts of the discourse and seem to be the Evangelist's summary of the whole chapter. The theme of testimony is picked up from the previous verses. The testimony is that of the "one from above." He alone speaks the words of God.

The metaphor of Jesus as the one sent from God has connections with Jewish legal terminology. A person's agent was to be considered identical with himself, and could act in the name of the person who sent him, since that person had handed over his affairs to the agent. Here (vv. 34f.) the Father has handed over all to the Son. But the Son is more than a prophet or envoy from God, since his revelation divides humanity into those who believe and have eternal life and those unbelievers who remain under judgment.

(Again, notice that eschatological judgment language is applied to Jesus' mission.) The real judgment occurs as people decide how they will respond to Jesus.

4. Disciples among the Non-Jews

The opening chapters showed Jesus gathering disciples among the Jews. Now he moves out to those who lived on the fringes of Judaism. The Samaritans, descendents of the Jewish and pagan population left in Samaria after the Assyrian conquest, revered Moses and the Torah but did not follow the views of "orthodox" Jews or center their worship in Jerusalem. Relationships between the two groups were extremely hostile. The royal official in the second story could have been a member of Herod's court. Members of the court would have been suspect as to their commitment to Judaism, since pagan influence was strong in court circles. The synoptic versions of the story suggest that a Gentile official was the recipient of the miracle.

John 4:1-15: *Jesus as Living Water*

The introduction (vv. 1-6) to the story of the Samaritan woman is awkward. Perhaps the Evangelist has put together earlier pieces of tradition about Jesus and John the Baptist with the introduction to this story. The Samaritan story contains further allusions to Christian baptism, which the Christian reader may see as expanding the water/spirit analogy from the Nicodemus story.

Jesus Baptizing

John 3:22 and 4:1 assert that Jesus himself engaged in a baptizing ministry. The Evangelist may have drawn that information from a traditional story which explained why Jesus abandoned that type of ministry and returns to Galilee to begin a different type of ministry. The story attributes his return to Galilee to Pharisaic opposition in Judea. The synoptic tradition links the beginning of Jesus' Galilean ministry with the death of the Baptist. It says nothing about any activity in Judea. Some scholars argue that the tradition reflected in John is historically plausible and also would explain why Jesus' disciples took up baptizing converts. (Matthew 28:19 attributes that practice to an explicit command of the risen Lord.) The parenthetical correction in verse 2 is seen as an attempt by the author or more likely (since 3:22 is not corrected), a later editor to bring the gospel in line with the common picture that Jesus never engaged in a baptizing ministry. Such a correction may have been one way of avoiding charges by later followers of the Baptist that Jesus was really only a disciple of John, who had gone off on his own, and not the Messiah. As it now stands in the gospel, this scene introduces the difference between the two types of baptism, that of John and that of the Christians. The story which follows will show the Christian reader that his baptism is different from that of John because it is not concerned with physical water but with the Spirit which bestows eternal life.

Location of the Story

Though the main route from Galilee to Judea lay through Samaria, other routes could have been taken through the Jordan valley. Therefore some exegetes read the "it was necessary" in verse 4 as an indication of divine necessity, just as the expression is used in the passion predictions. The location of the well, Sychar, has been questioned since the time of St. Jerome, since there is no town in the area.

Jacob's well near Shechem may be the intended location.

The Living Water

Johannine stories frequently begin, as this one does, with an initiative by Jesus. This story is carefully divided into scenes by changes in conversation partners. But throughout the story there is a collection of Christological titles which progressively reveal Jesus' true identity. We saw that John used a similar chain of titles to link the discipleship stories in the first chapter.

At first, the woman identifies herself and Jesus in ethnic terms. The Evangelist has added a parenthetical remark (verse 9b) to remind us of the significance of that distinction: Jews and Samaritans would have nothing to do with each other. He knows that he must explain how a Jewish Messiah can be the Savior of non-Jews. The synoptics limit Jesus' ministry to Jews or Gentiles close to Judaism. John portrays the Gentile acceptance of Jesus, which Paul and Acts show to have been a dominant feature of the early mission, as prefigured in the ministry of Jesus (10:16, sheep not of this fold; 12:20, Greeks come to Jesus).

Jesus says that the woman does not know who is speaking—a motif that occurs frequently in John. Believers come to find out who Jesus is when they encounter him as the disciples did in the first chapter. Nonbelievers reject Jesus because they never come to realize his true identity, but continue to identify him in human terms of family, local origin, occupation—teacher, true/false prophet—or race, as the woman does here. As long as a person sees Jesus in these categories, he or she does not believe. If the woman really knew who was speaking to her, she would have asked for the gift of God, the living (= flowing) water.

Judaism used both expressions, "living water" and "gift

of God," to refer to the Torah. The OT (cf. Sir 24:21) compares the wisdom of God with water. The Johannine reader will also recall the water/spirit parallel from the Nicodemus story (3:5) and the allusions to baptism, which the Evangelist has heightened by interlocking both of these stories with material about John the Baptist.

As in the Nicodemus story, the woman does not understand the symbolic meaning of Jesus' words, but asks how Jesus thinks he is going to get water out of the well. Her sarcastic "Are you greater than Jacob?" is an example of Johannine irony. Without knowing or intending it, she has made a true statement about Jesus: he is greater than Jacob. (Since there is no OT story about Jacob giving his descendents a well, exegetes assume that John draws upon Jewish haggadic traditions. Perhaps those traditions influenced the allusion to Jacob's dream in the Son-of-Man saying which concluded the discipleship stories of chapter 1, where Jesus, the Son of Man, has been identified with the ladder of the vision. Thus he is clearly greater than the patriarch, Jacob.)

When Jesus claims that he gives the water of eternal life, he makes it clear that he is claiming to be greater than Jacob and that he is speaking symbolically. (John 7:37–39 indicates that the "living water" given by Jesus refers to the Spirit.) The woman's reply shows that either she does not understand Jesus' claim at all or that she understands but responds with sarcasm to indicate disbelief, saying something like "While you're at it, provide indoor plumbing."

John 4:16–42 *Jesus as Savior of the World*

Jesus Is the True Prophet

Since the discourse about the water "failed," Jesus switches

back to the literal level (v. 16). The Samaritan legal situation
is unknown (Jewish law permitted three wives); so it is
difficult to tell whether Jesus' description of the woman's
husbands implies condemnation or is a demonstration that
he has unusual knowledge of the woman's personal life. We
saw in 2:25 that Jesus' knowledge of what was in people's
hearts implied knowledge of their religious and moral disposition. The previous chapter explained that some people
do not believe in Jesus because their actions are contrary
to the commands of God. Therefore it would not be impossible to argue that the Evangelist is using this story to
exemplify what happens when a person comes to the light:
The woman's deeds are exposed. She is now convinced that
Jesus is a prophet.

The Samaritans expected that a prophet like Moses would
come in the last days and decide questions about worship
that were hotly debated between Samaritans and Jews (v.
20), she may have had the Mosaic prophet in mind. The
Jews had destroyed the Samaritan temple on Mt. Gerezim
in 128 B.C., but the Samaritans had continued to worship
on the traditional site.

Jesus' answer (v. 21) insists that salvation (= himself)
comes from the Jews but he rejects both the Jewish and
the Samaritan claims to possess the true place of worship
for the messianic age.

In Spirit and Truth

The expression "in spirit and truth" is a Semitic hendiadys
meaning "Spirit of truth" or "true spirit." It cannot be
construed to mean that John rejects external worship. The
"Spirit of truth" the Spirit of God (v. 24), which was
thought to establish a new, purified people of God in the

Note the combination of seeing the light of life, cleansing and renewal by the holy spirit, flowing water, keeping the words of God, and renewed worship of God.

The following passage speaks of the knowledge and glory that the new people will have in the last days:

> . . . The truth shall arise in the world forever; for the world has defiled itself in the way of wickedness under the dominion of Perversity until the time of the last judgment. Then God will cleanse by his truth all the works of every man . . . and he will cause the Spirit of Truth to gush forth upon him like lustral water . . . the just will comprehend the knowledge of the most high and the perfect of way will have understanding of the wisdom of the sons of angels. For God has chosen them for an everlasting covenant and all the glory of the Man is theirs [I QS IV 19b–23a].

These passages help clarify how John's words might have been understood by his contemporaries. His gospel has often messianic age. The following passages from the community rule of the Essenes show how these expectations were connected in contemporary Judaism.

> . . . by the spirit of true counsel concerning the ways of man shall all his sins be atoned when he beholds the light of life. By the holy spirit of the community, in his truth, shall he be cleansed of all his sins; and by the spirit of uprightness and humility shall his iniquity be atoned. By his soul's humility toward all the precepts of God shall his flesh be cleansed with the lustral water and sanctified in flowing water. And he shall establish his steps to walk perfectly in all the ways of God, according to his command, concerning his regular feasts; and he shall step neither to the right nor to the left and shall make no single step from all his words [I QS III 6b–11a].

about the community of believers; yet these parallels to his language come from the rulebook of the Qumran community. They suggest to us that much of John's language—for example, that about flowing water within the believer—would have been understood to describe those who had joined what, for the Evangelist, is the eschatological community, the Christian community. Unlike the community at Qumran, this community will not be an exclusive group within Judaism, focused on keeping the law and a purified cult. Rather, as this story goes on to show, it may include anyone—even Samaritans—among those who have been cleansed by the Spirit and worship the Father in spirit and truth.

The woman responds to Jesus' teaching on worship by claiming that the Samaritans expect the Messiah to teach them such things (v. 25). Jesus tells her that he is the Messiah. Verse 24 is the last time the term Messiah is given to Jesus by a believer. From the next chapter on, whenever the term appears it will be as the focus of debate and controversy about Jesus' identity.

The term Messiah is itself ambiguous. First-century Judaism had a variety of images of what the Messiah would be like. This story makes it clear that Jesus did not literally fulfill many of those expectations. Whenever "Messiah" is used, the Evangelist usually has the discussion go beyond that title to another designation. Those who seek to restrict the terms of God's salvation to their own expectations for the Messiah find themselves opposed to Jesus. The believer will allow God's salvation to be defined by the terms of Jesus' revelation.

John 4:27-38 *The Disciples and the Mission of Jesus*

Although the disciples began intensive missionary activity

only after the resurrection, all the gospels have some scene in which the earthly Jesus sends them on a mission (Mk 6:7-13 parr.). This scene is John's parallel to that tradition. We find the closest synoptic parallel to the saying about the plentiful harvest (v. 35b) associated with the sending out of the disciples in Mt 9:37f. and Lk 10:2.

Verses 27-30 provide a transition to the discussion of the disciples' mission. The woman responds as we have learned from chapter 1 that a believer should: she goes out to call others to Jesus. Here, her activity is analogous to that of later Christian missionaries. John 4:30 has Samaritans coming from the city to meet Jesus, and their coming provides the backdrop for Jesus' instructions about the mission.

Typically, the dialogue between Jesus and the disciples begins with misunderstanding. Jesus uses "food" to refer to his own mission in accomplishing the will of the Father (cf. 5:36, 6:38). The verses which follow describe the Christian mission by reinterpreting two proverbial statements to make it clear that Jesus' ministry initiates the eschatological harvest. Verses 34-36 claim that the traditional four months between sowing and harvest will not occur. A similar metaphor is found in the OT. Leviticus 26:5 says that, in the Promised Land, threshing, vintage, and sowing will be so plentiful that they will overlap. Amos 9:13 has converted that image into one of the salvation to come. John 4:36 takes up that traditional image.

Verse 37 takes up another proverb, which usually appears as a pessimistic comment on the futility of human endeavors (e.g., Mi 6:15). But here it provides the point of departure for Jesus' commissioning the disciples for the harvest, which the previous proverbs make clear is to be one of joy. Commentators are divided over the identity of the "others," suggesting John the Baptist, Jesus, the Father, a twofold mission along the lines of Acts 8, or the OT prophets as possibilities. Since the disciples will later be formally commissioned as Jesus' agents, we consider him the most likely referent. However, the Evangelist may have simply used the proverb as a generalization for any and all earlier bringers of God's word.

John 4:39–42 *Savior of the World*

The concluding verses provide a striking contrast to the superficial faith of the Jews (2:23–25). Perhaps the Evangelist had the early success of the mission to Samaria (cf. Acts 8) in mind when he spoke of the many believers there. As in the first chapter, the new converts must move from believing on the basis of someone else's testimony to their own experience of Jesus. The request that he remain (v. 40) indicates that they become true disciples (cf. 1:39).

The story culminates with the confession that Jesus is Savior of the world. That confession shows that the particularism of a Jewish or Samaritan Messiah has been transcended. "Savior" was not a Jewish messianic title but it was widely used in early Christianity (Lk 2:11, Acts 5:31, 11:23, 1 Jn 4:14, 2 Tm 1:10). Some scholars suppose that it was taken from OT references to Yahweh as Savior (Ps 24:5, Is 12:2, cp. Lk 1:47); others, that Gentile Christians derived it from the widely used language that praised kings for their benefits to a city or people. The NT uses the title in contexts which know the OT usage, but the same writings also show contact with Hellenistic thought and language. The OT passages probably provided the scriptural basis for using a title which could be understood in a wider context. Thus "Savior" provided an expression of Jesus' significance that was not limited by the boundaries of Jewish religious terminology. In this story it is a title which can unite Jew and Samaritan in a single confession, rather than separate them.

Christianity and Non-Christian Religions

Christians today still have to ask how Jesus can be the Savior of people who come from cultural and religious traditions quite different from those of the West. Many people have understood religious pluralism to imply that all ways of salvation are about equal. People may select what suits their temperament or is congenial to their cultural and religious heritage. Sustained theological discussion of this problem is still lacking in Christian circles. Vatican II's decree on non-Christian religions merely lays out basic guidelines for dialogue with other religious traditions. First, all religions respond to basic human ontological structures, which dictate that humanity will seek the absolute, the meaning of life. Second, in their dialogue with other religions, Catholics should preserve and promote the spiritual and moral good in other religions, societies, and cultures. These guidelines do not presuppose that all religious traditions are equivalent. To some, they may even appear covertly "imperialistic." Christianity is to be the standard for moral and spiritual good.

Of course, this question of standards, criteria, and discernment is ultimately at stake in any dialogue that is to get beyond pleasantries and mutual back-scratching. The NT clearly claims that Jesus is the Savior of the world and not just of the Jews. Especially in the gospel of John, we see that this claim required a process of assimilating and reformulating Hellenistic religious language and concepts, both Jewish and pagan, so that they could express the Christian vision. The dialogue reflected in these pages is mutual, though not always friendly where Judaism is involved. The non-Christian is ultimately required to convert. But, on the Christian side, we witness a genuine process of new formulation and understanding of the significance of Jesus.

Dialogue is not simply making translations of the old

Jewish religious language into some new language so that the message remains unchanged. Rather, John shows the ability to forge genuinely new symbols and language from the confluence of Jewish religious language, Hellenistic religious language, and the earlier Christian traditions that he inherited. At the same time, he remains critical of these various traditions. Not everything can be retained as one moves to new understanding. Jesus is not simply the fulfillment of any or all of the religious expectations of Jew, Samaritan, or Greek; he also transforms them—which often requires the convert to make substantial modifications in his or her earlier understanding of religious truth. The Evangelist realizes that people often cannot bring themselves to abandon deeply held religious convictions. He frequently alludes to the mysterious character of faith and he is aware that even some who begin to believe in Jesus may find themselves scandalized and turn back.

The story of the Samaritan woman is an interesting model of this process. Jesus admits to being the prophet/Messiah expected by the Samaritans, but he rejects certain Samaritan beliefs about the Messiah. He will not prove that they are right in their dispute with the Jews over where to worship God; both groups lose that point. Further, their hatred of Jews must bow to the inevitable fact that Jesus is a Jew. But the confession which concludes the episode is neither Samaritan nor Jewish; it includes both, and the Gentiles as well.

John 4:43–45 *Reaction in Galilee*

Despite the striking success in Samaria, we are not allowed to forget that Jesus encountered opposition. Verse 43 is transitional, and typical of the Evangelist's method of locating a scene by giving some temporal and geographical marker, however imprecise (cf. 4:3b, 46). The traditional saying in verse 44 is preserved in several variations (Mk 6:4, Lk 4:24, POxy I, 6 = GTh 31). The combination of this saying with a statement about apparent success (v. 45) has led some exegetes to claim that John thinks Jesus' true homeland is Judea. That suggestion is contrary to John's clear emphasis on Jesus' Galilean origins (1:46, 2:1, 7:42, 52, 19:9). Others think the saying was added to the gospel later. Both views falter before the Markan tradition, which contains the rejection saying and juxtaposes it with apparent success. Luke combines the rejection saying with a miracle similar to the one Jesus is about to work in Capernaum. We find many traditions similar to Mark in this gospel. Therefore, it seems likely that the Evangelist derived the juxtaposition of success/rejection at Galilee, followed by a miracle at Capernaum, from his tradition. The Evangelist's assessment of faith based on miracles, in 2:23-25, suggests that he would negatively understand the "success" mentioned in verse 45, just as he will include a warning about such faith in the following miracle story (v. 48).

John 4:46-54 *The Royal Official's Son*

The "call stories" end in Galilee with the cure of a royal official's son, which is similar to a synoptic story about the healing of the centuion's slave (Mt 8:5-13, Lk 7:1-10). Though the two versions differ on many details, they seem to be variations on the same incident. The synoptics have understood the story as one which demonstrates the willingness of the Gentiles to believe, as contrasted with the rejection Jesus receives from the Jews. John leaves the status of the man—Jew or Gentile—unclear. The association of this story with that about the conversion of the Samaritans suggests that he understands the official to represent those who are outside the religious orbit of official Judaism.

Like the other miracle stories, John seems to have taken this one from a collection; note the numbering in verse 54. The language of the story is not peculiarly Johannine. As in the Cana story, Jesus appears to reject the petition that he work the miracle (v. 48, cp. 2:4). Like the other miracle stories, John tells this one in such a way as to stress the effectiveness of Jesus' word. He shows little interest in the miraculous cure itself. The expression "he and his whole household thereupon became believers" (v. 53b) reflects the missionary language of early Christianity (Acts 10:2, 11:14, 16:5). The collection of miracles from which the Evangelist derived this story may have been used in missionary preaching.

Although there have been suggestions since the opening verses of the gospel (e.g., 1:5) that Jesus will be rejected and some indication that larger audiences heard Jesus, these first chapters have been largely private encounters between Jesus and a disciple or disciples. They show all types of people coming to believe in Jesus. The two miracles lead people to believe in Jesus—which is not true of later miracles, which create hostility and division. This generally positive assessment provides the reader with a foundation—perhaps a reaffirmation of his or her own faith—on which to turn to the controversy material in the next section of the work. From now on, Jesus will be increasingly embroiled in controversy and hostility. His opponents will bring objections against Christian belief, which the Evangelist wishes to show are false objections, stemming from blindness, ill will, hostility to God's revelation, and sin. The intensity of debate in these chapters suggests that the arguments that were brought forward were serious challenges to the faith of Christians in

John's day. We even see some people renounce their belief. As Jesus meets each challenge, the Christian reader learns how he or she should respond in a similar situation so as to defend and secure the faith to which he or she must testify, for, as we have seen, the true believer bears witness to Jesus.

The Sequence of Chapters 4 to 6

Chapter 4 ends in Galilee; chapter 5 begins at an unnamed feast in Jerusalem; chapter 6 takes place back in Galilee, without any indication of Jesus' having returned there. In chapter 7, Jesus returns to Jerusalem for a feast. Further, 7:21 refers to events described in chapter 5. Many interpreters seek to solve this geographical juggling by supposing that the Evangelist originally had chapter 6 after chapter 4. They point out that such an arrangement would bring John more in line with the synoptic tradition, which has an extended Galilean ministry followed by that in Jerusalem. Further, the parallel to Mk 6 in 4:43ff. would then come directly before a whole section of material (with parallels in Mk 6 and 8) which is found in chapter 6.

In addition, Louis Martyn (*History*, pp. 49–50) has advanced a structural argument that links the composition of chapters 5 and 7. He compares the sequence of events that follow the two Jerusalem miracles in chapters 5 and 9 and finds the following pattern:

Traditional healing	5:1–9b	9:1–7
Dramatic expansion	9c–15	8–41
Jesus' sermon	19–47	10:1–18
Opinion divided	7:11–13	19–21
Exchange at feast	14–24	22–30

Violence	25–30	31–39
Believers	31	40–42
Authorities act	32–52	11:45ff.

This pattern suggests that what may look like a random stringing together of incidents represents a careful plan of composition. In the present ordering of the gospel, each sequence is interrupted once by a major body of material centered on "life." Chapter 6, on the bread of life, interrupts the first. The Lazarus miracle interrupts the second. We suggest that Martyn's pattern is derived from units the Evangelist composed prior to the writing of the gospel.

The difficulty with theories of rearrangement is that there is no manuscript evidence of such changes. The earliest manuscripts have the traditional order. Nor has anyone given a convincing explanation of why or how these chapters were arranged. We suppose that the structural ties between chapters 4 and 6 and the pattern of Galilean ministry, followed by Jerusalem activity, were all part of the traditional material the Evangelist used. He himself is responsible for the elaborate parallels between chapters 5, 7, and 9–10. The present arrangement of the gospel may follow a plan similar to this one:

1. *Chs. 1–4:* Calling and preliminary instruction of the disciples, framed by the two Cana miracles—the last a successful healing
2. *Chs. 5–12:* Public preaching initiated by an unsuccessful healing; the person does not believe and the following controversy ends in rejection
3. *Chs. 13–17:* Final, private instruction of the disciples
4. *Chs. 18–21:* Crucifixion/resurrection, the glorification of Jesus.

The healing miracle which concludes chapter 4 and that which begins chapter 5 provide a striking contrast and clearly indicate that the character of response to Jesus has shifted. The relocation also allows John to lengthen the time period of the ministry. He will do the same with the Jerusalem material, from chapter 7 on, by breaking up units that appear to discuss the same topic into discourses that will be delivered at different feasts. This extended period of activity, in Galilee and in Jerusalem, leaves Jesus' opponents without excuses. He has shown them "many works from the Father" that should have led them to believe that he is indeed sent by God. As a result of the lengthened time period, the hostility against Jesus takes the form of an extended plot. For John, the death of Jesus cannot be understood as an accident which resulted from a misunderstanding of deeds and teachings in a brief period of time.

PART TWO

Public Ministry

5. The Authority of Jesus

With this chapter, the gospel turns to controversies surrounding Jesus. Recent studies have stressed that many of these debates must represent the type of controversy between Christians and Jews in John's day. This feature is clear at the end of the chapter, where the question raised by Jesus' healing on the Sabbath is not his authority to heal but his claim to stand in a special relationship to God. The Christian reader would recognize Jewish objections to his belief that Jesus is the Son of God. Thus these stories played an important role for John's readers. They could learn, from the parallels between Jesus' experience and their own, how to answer their adversaries in similar situations. Jesus' answers will keep their faith from being shaken when people challenge them.

John 5:1-18 *Healing of the Paralytic*

John introduces an unnamed feast as the setting for this incident. Although there is no close parallel to the healing elsewhere in the tradition, its language and style suggest that the Evangelist took the story from his miracle collection. Most interpreters think that verses 2-3, 5-9, and perhaps 13-14 come from that source. Verse 9 indicates that the original story was a Sabbath controversy (cp. the healing of a paralytic in Lk 13:10-17). Jesus' injunction in verse 14 suggests the healing/forgiveness connection in the Lucan story (Lk 13:12). Unlike the previous two stories, in which Jesus was asked to perform a miracle, here, and in the stories which follow, he takes the initiative. (A similar initiative occurs in the Lucan story.)

If the Lucan story is something like what John found in his source, the Sabbath miracle should culminate in a saying of Jesus. A saying such as that in verse 14 may have been expanded by the Evangelist into the scene in verses 10–18 to serve as an introduction to the longer discourse which is the real message of the chapter. Both this story and its parallel in chapter 9 issue in a similar series of events: the person in confronted by authorities who are investigating the healing; Jesus seeks out the person and makes a pronouncement; Jesus makes a pronouncement against the authorities.

Verses 16–18 introduce the discourse which follows. In synoptic controversy stories, Jesus defends himself either on humanitarian grounds (e.g., Lk 13:15) or on the basis of his authority (Mk 2:28). Here, Jesus appeals to his relationship with the Father (cp. the appeal to the OT in Mt 12:5). He argues for his actions on the basis of what God does. Jews held that God could not have ceased work completely on the Sabbath; since people are born and die on the Sabbath, his providence must still be active and he must continue to judge. The language in which verse 19 draws the implications of this claim suggests the later position of the Church: Jesus is said to have "dissolved" the Sabbath rule, not merely to have broken it. Further, he is claiming equality with God. The discourse now explains the relationship between him and the Father.

John 5:19–30 *Jesus Acts as the Father Does*

Jesus defends himself against the charge that he is blasphemously claiming equality with God, but his activities—giving life (v. 21) and judging (v. 22)—parallel the activities of God on the Sabbath. John constantly uses the metaphor of Jesus as God's agent, derived from legal terminology. An agent was considered identical with the one who sent him; he could make binding agreements in the name of the person who sent him, and was entitled to all the honors and privileges of the one who commissioned him (cf. v. 23). John takes over this language to explain the identity between Jesus and the Father, who sent him, without involving himself in speculation about the ontological relationship between the two, such as later troubled Christians. At the same time, Jesus is also "Son." Thus his status as "sent by the Father" is more than that which might be attributed to an OT prophet.

Commentators have advanced many theories about the "greater works" referred to in 20b. John has used similar expressions at 1:50 ("greater things") and 3:12 ("heavenly things"). The immediately following sentences give the content of the "greater things." Therefore, it seems likely that the phrase refers to Jesus as the one who gives life and who judges. The previous examples would also lead us to expect a Son-of-Man saying at this point and a reference to the crucifixion/exaltation of Jesus, which is part of his life-giving activity (3:14f.). The Son-of-Man saying at 3:14f. is followed by a section on the judgment brought by Jesus' presence. He stresses the priority of the life-giving activity of Jesus over judgment. The latter is consistently portrayed as the inevitable outcome of the fact that some people will reject Jesus. This order reverses that of apocalyptic texts, where judgment of the wicked is a necessary preliminary to new life for the faithful.

Like the passage in chapter 3, the first description of Jesus, life-giving activity (vv. 21–16) is written from the perspective of "realized eschatology"—language about final judgment and eternal life is not located in the future but is applied to the present. Judgment or eternal life is determined by whether a person believes in Jesus and accepts his revelation of the Father.

Verses 27–29 shift to the perspective of a future judgment, and there are several peculiarities in these verses. "Son of Man" is used without an article and is described as judging. Although statements about the Son of Man as judge were used very early in Christianity—if not by Jesus himself—John does not speak of the Son of Man acting as judge. That is Jesus' function as Son of God. "Dead" in verse 25 referred to living people; here it refers to those in their graves. Verse 25 suggests that only the righteous awaken (cp. Dn 12:1–3), while verse 29 presumes that the wicked are raised as well. "Hour" in verse 25 refers to the present time of Jesus' ministry; in verse 28 it refers to the future. Such discrepancies between this passage and the verses preceding it have led many to suggest that a final editor added these verses to the gospel in order to make it clear that the Evangelist's "realized eschatology" does not invalidate Christian tradition about a final judgment.

We suggest that the Evangelist has incorporated verses 27–29 as a deliberate contrast to the previous verses. The clue lies in the parallel expressions "to your great wonderment" (verse 20) and "no need for you to be amazed" (v. 28), which some include in their list of discordant elements. The previous examples, discussed in connection with verse 20, showed that John always follows up references to "greater things" with an example of what he means. In the earlier passages he preceded "greater things" with some "earthly things" which everyone should accept. Here, he has reversed that order. The understanding of eschatological language in the previous verses may be difficult, but everyone would agree with the statement in verses 27–29. Since these verses depart from the language and style of the

Evangelist, he is probably quoting a traditional saying in his community.

Today many people are disturbed by those who preach that the world is about to end. Some wonder how Christians are to relate to the many eschatological predictions in the NT. Others are frightened or put off by the highly judgmental picture of God that is part of such preaching. John offers some helpful pointers for understanding eschatology. First, the primary emphasis is not on God as judge but upon God's love for the world and his desire to save. Jesus did not come to condemn people but to bring them life; he is anxious to reach out to them. Second, the crucial point is not some cosmic judgment in the future—though John is not denying that belief—but the present, in which a person either accepts and keeps Jesus' word or rejects it. The believer need not fear the final judgment, since he or she has already passed from death to life.

John 5:31–47 *Witnesses to Jesus*

The Evangelist now turns to the legal language of witness and testimony. In the opening chapters of the gospel, testimony played an important part in bringing disciples to Jesus. Now that the narrative has turned to controversy, testimony is legal testimony to Jesus against opponents.

The True Witnesses to Jesus

Both biblical (cf. Dt 19:15) and rabbinic law prohibited a person from testifying on his own behalf, and Jesus claims that he can produce other witnesses. First, he refers to John the Baptist (vv. 33–35; cf. 1:19–34). But such human testimony is of less importance than the divine witnesses whom Jesus will call next. He first employs human testimony and then, in the pattern we have seen elsewhere (e.g., 1:50-51), moves from that lesser testimony to the greater. First, he points to his ministry, the works given him by the Father (v. 36). Then the Father himself is invoked as witness.

Some commentators suppose this testimony to be internal; however, the previous two examples referred to external events viewed in the light of faith. Therefore, we are inclined toward the view that the reference to Scripture in the next verse indicates what Jesus means by calling the Father as witness. The expression "search the Scripture" was a technical term for studying Scripture. Here, as elsewhere, Jesus accuses his opponents of misreading God's revelation in Scripture.

Failure to Accept Jesus' Witnesses

Jesus began his list of witnesses by denying the need of human testimony. Now he begins his denunciation of those who do not believe by denying the need for human glory ("praise," NAB). But while the previous statement was followed with a conditional acceptance of human testimony, Jesus cannot accept human glory from those who do not honor the Father because they do not accept his agent. The expression "those who come in their own names" (v. 43) is used of false prophets in the OT (Jer 29:25, 31). Jesus is not a false prophet or sinner, as his opponents think, but God's agent and, as such, is entitled to all the honor due the Father who sent him.

The concluding verses of this prophetic condemnation are bitterly sarcastic. Jewish tradition held that Moses would intercede for Israel at the judgment, but this entire section attributes failure to believe in Jesus to failure to love the God in whom his opponents claim they believe. Jesus tells them that if they cannot hear God's testimony in Scripture, they can hardly expect to find Moses as their intercessor before God. He will in fact condemn them.

The Jews as Opponents in the Fourth Gospel

The "controversy stories" from this point on are very harsh in their language about the Jews—the term is often symbolic of all that is hostile to Jesus and God. Sometimes Christians have taken such language as grounds for prejudice against—or worse, persecution of—Jewish people. When reading passages such as these, we should remember that many of the Christians for whom John wrote had probably been Jews. They would not have understood that Jews are cast as the protagonists in the gospel to imply racial prejudice against Jews.

In fact, John's community was close enough to Judaism to have been affected by the exclusion of Christians from the synagogue in A.D. 90. They obviously engaged in debate with fellow Jews in their attempts to gain converts. Secondly, these verses were written in a situation in which Christians— not Jews—were an oppressed minority, struggling to survive. Jewish opponents argued that Jesus could not have been the Messiah predicted in Scripture (e.g., 8:52, 12:32), and may even have persuaded some to abandon Christianity. Therefore it was important for the community to have an image of Judaism that would enable them to withstand such pressures. Consequently, the Jews are consistently portrayed as opposed to God and totally unable to understand his revelation.

Today, Christians have no reason to propagate such an

image. Both the Pope and the World Council of Churches have condemned the use of anti-Semitic language by Christians. Instead, Christians are encouraged to appreciate the positive contributions to our understanding of God made by the Jews.

6. Jesus as the Bread of Life

The controversy that develops in this chapter centers on a fundamental Christian institution, the Eucharist. It will even cost Jesus some of his followers. The entire chapter is based on a skeleton of traditional material which parallels the sequence of events in Mark:

1. Loaves miracle	Jn 6: 1–15	Mk 6:30–40
2. Walks on water	16–21	45–54
3. Request for sign	22–34	Mk 8:11–13
4. Debate on Jesus' parentage	41–44	Mk 6: 1–6
5. Disciples misunderstand	60–65	Mk 8:16–21
6. Peter's confession	66–69	27–30
7. Passion prediction	70–71	30–33

The major Johannine expansion of this skeleton is the lengthy discourse on the bread of life (vv. 35–59).

John 6:1–15 *The Loaves Miracle*

Most exegetes think that John has added the following to his source: "later on"; "of Tiberias" (v. 1); verse 2b; verse 4; "to Philip" for "to the disciples" (vv. 5, 7); verse 6; "so that nothing will perish" ("go to waste," NAB; v. 12); "saw the sign he performed"; "undoubtedly"; who is to come into the world" (v. 14).

The story of the miraculous feeding occurs in all four gospels and early Christian tradition associated it with the Eucharist. (Catacomb art regularly links the two.) The Johannine version has heightened eucharistic allusions when compared with the synoptics. Jesus is the one who takes the initiative in feeding the people. He distributes the bread himself. Gathering the fragments so that nothing would perish may also reflect eucharistic praxis (the NAB obscures this allusion by translating v. 12b as "go to waste"). The Evangelist locates this miracle at the time of the Passover (v. 4), and the discourse which follows it will draw heavily on Exodus motifs.

In the Johannine version, the crowd responds by proclaiming Jesus the prophet and trying to make him king. Popular Jewish expectations held that a prophet like Moses would come in the last days. (The Essenes at Qumran seem to have looked upon the unknown priest who founded their sect as "the prophet.") Often the prophet was expected to perform three signs: give bread in the wilderness; produce living (= running) water, and ride on a donkey. John is the only gospel which portrays Jesus as fulfilling all three expectations—though not literally in the case of water (4:14, 7:38). The crowd's response is based on the literal expectation of such a prophet to rule over Israel. (The passion narrative will explain the sense in which Jesus may be said to be king.) Jesus refuses to be the type of messiah-king they desire. He does not fit into the mold of many such popular messianic expectations, and his failure to do so is an important part of the controversy in this gospel. Throughout the work, the Evangelist insists that Jesus fulfills Jewish messianic expectations by transcending them: the Son of Man is greater than Moses, and even Abraham was glad to see his day.

John 6:16-20 *Walking on Water*

John's version of this story is much less detailed than

its synoptic counterparts. It seems closer to a simple nature miracle, and there is no comment on the disciples' interpretation of the vision or on their faith. On the other hand, "and Jesus had still not joined them" (cf v. 17b) may indicate that the Evangelist thinks his readers already knew the story.

The phrase by which Jesus identifies himself to the frightened disciples, literally "I am" (NAB: "It is I"), has a double significance. It can be simply a self-identification, but John uses such "I am" sayings without any predicate several times (cf. 8:24, 58, 13:19, 18:5). Many of these seem to be a claim to the divine name "I AM," found in the OT (Ex 20:5, Dt 5:5-9, Is 43:10, 44:6). Here, the storm stops as soon as Jesus pronounces the divine name. The miraculous response of nature continues when the boat arrives instantaneously at its destination. Although he has not worked this story into the Passover motifs of the rest of the chapter, and may have abbreviated it, the Evangelist probably retains it in its traditional place as a counterpoint to the various misunderstandings of Jesus in this chapter.

John 6:25-34 *Request for a Sign*

Because the sea miracle has separated Jesus and the crowd, the Evangelist supplies a rather complex account of how they found Jesus again (vv. 22-24). The traditional story of the demand that Jesus give a sign follows. John has expanded that story to tie it into the bread-of-life theme. Rather than a sign to prove his authority, the crowd asks Jesus for the same sign they have already witnessed, but did not understand, as fulfilling the promise of manna.

Jesus' words to the crowd are full of the double meanings that are characteristic of Johannine discourse. Literal observation of the miracle is rejected in favor of "seeing" the sign—John's code for understanding the symbolic or theological significance of what has taken place (v. 26). Reception of physical food is as irrelevant as the water in the well in chapter 4. What is important is "doing the works of God," which Jesus further defines as believing that he is the one sent by the Father (vv. 27–29). The crowd correctly understands that he demands that they believe in him, and challenges him to prove that he is indeed God's agent. Not realizing that he has already done so, they want him to provide manna, as Moses did. The rest of the discourse casts the crowd as the Israelites under Moses, who murmured against him in the desert.

Jesus' opponents initiate the discourse by citing the passage from Scripture which they expect him to fulfill. The debate over the proper understanding of that text, which follows, looks very much like the kind of apologetic argument that would have been carried on in John's community. Jesus rejects the Jews' understanding of the passage. *Moses did not give bread from heaven, but the Father gives* it (present tense). Nor is there to be a literal repeat of the Exodus miracle. Rather, one should look for its fulfillment in what comes down from heaven and gives life to the world (v. 33). The reader knows that that role is filled by Jesus; but the crowd fails to understand and—much like the Samaritan woman and the water (4:15)—demands a permanent supply of bread (v. 34).

John 6:35–59 *Discourse on the Bread of Life*

The complex weaving together of symbols and allusions in this discourse could hardly have been understood by Jews of either John's or Jesus' day, but it speaks clearly to the

Christian reader. Doubtless the picture of literal-minded Jews who do not understand their own Scripture coincides with the experience Christians had in their debates with the Jews. Not only will the Jews reject Jesus, they will persecute those who believe in him.

Structure and Style of the Discourse

Recent studies of Jewish homiletic technique have suggested that this section is cast in that style. Jesus' opponents have provided the text for the sermon: "he gave us bread from heaven to eat" (v. 31). The preacher was expected to comment on that text word for word and to bring in other OT citations as part of the exposition. Jesus has already explained that "he gave" should not be understood to mean "Moses gave" but the "Father gives." Now he explains the rest of the citation. The discourse gives two separate treatments of the bread of life. Verses 35–51a make the bread a symbol of the teaching of Jesus. Then verses 51b–59 give a eucharistic interpretation. This second discourse may serve to explicate the final words of the OT text, "to eat."

Bread from Heaven as the Teaching of Jesus

The first section of the discourse makes the bread a symbol of the teaching of Jesus. A common Jewish tradition compares the law, divine wisdom, and the word of God to food (cf. Am 8:11–13, Prv 9:5, Sir 15:3, 24:21). Jesus opens this discourse by declaring that he is both the bread and the living water expected of the Messiah (v. 35). The crowd, behaving like their ancestors under Moses, murmurs against Jesus and refuses to believe (v. 36).

Verses 37–40 are a solemn declaration by Jesus that belief in him as Son of Man is necessary for anyone who expects to share the resurrection of the righteous on the last day. At the same time, he suggests that God must draw people to faith: "all that the Father gives to me shall come to me" (v. 37).

Such language should not be read to imply that some people are damned because God does not give them the opportunity to believe. Rather, it stems from the very real experiences of persecution and rejection which the early Christians suffered. They could not take all the credit for the fact that they were able to believe in such circumstances. When Jesus continues, "no one who comes will I ever reject," he is probably contrasting the Christian willingness to accept anyone who believes in Jesus with the experience which Christians had just suffered, around the time the gospel was written. The Jews rejected them, formally excommunicating Christians from the synagogue in A.D. 90. The insistence that the Father must draw people to Jesus may also have consoled the early Christians when people rejected their preaching. They could take such rejection as part of God's plan.

Another traditional piece, the question of Jesus' origin (vv. 41–44), provides a dialogue to take up another section of the quotation, "from heaven." The story has been recast in typical Johannine language. The truth about Jesus' origins is unrecognized by his protagonists: He is the one sent from heaven, but his opponents cannot see that because they think only of his earthly family, not of his divine mission. Jesus returns to his assertion that God is the one who draws people to him. In proper homiletic style, he quotes Is 54:13, "they shall be taught by God" (v. 45), to prove his point.

The final verses of this section (46–51a) contrast Jesus as the bread which gives eternal life with the manna in the OT, which did not give eternal life but only preserved the physical life of the people. Jesus is also implicitly contrasted with Moses. Jewish tradition held that Moses had been privileged to "see God." Some Jewish authors in the first century even describe Israel as a special nation because she has been privileged to see God. Jesus denies that claim. Anyone who really knows the Father will come to him. He is the only one who has seen God (v. 46).

The Eucharistic Bread

Verse 51b takes a new turn, which many see as exegeting the final phrase of the quotation, "to eat." The bread is identified as the flesh of Jesus, which will convey life to the world. Many interpreters think that verse 53 represents the eucharistic formula as it was known in John's community. Although it is not the same as the words of institution reported in the synoptics or Paul, it is found elsewhere in early Christianity (Ignatius, *Rom* 7:3; *Phila* 6:1; Justin, *Apol* I, 66). The reference to drinking blood in this formula would have been highly offensive to Jewish ears. Even today in kosher Jewish homes, meat, before it is cooked, is carefully soaked to draw out any blood, since the OT law expressly forbids the eating of blood. Contrast this formula with that in Mt 26:26ff., which is carefully worded to avoid such offensive language.

As in the earlier discourse, the eucharistic bread is contrasted with the manna eaten by the Jews in the wilderness. The latter did not preserve those who ate it from death, or from displeasing God. This contrast between the death of the Israelites in the wilderness and the life given to Christians, the new Israel, was a common theme of early Christian preaching. Paul uses the fate of the Israelites who ate manna and drank living water but still displeased God as a warning to the Corinthians that they must be concerned about their conduct as Christians (1 Cor 10). In Hebrews 3, the story of the wilderness generation is a warning to Christians not to fall away from their faith, as those in the wilderness had done. John is using the comparison to contrast Christ and his salvation with that offered by Moses. Those who continue to follow Moses are condemned to death—a theme that will be elaborated in chapter 8. While we might expect the Jews to reject this exaltation of Jesus over Moses, this chapter concludes with an even more serious scene of rejection: some of Jesus' followers abandon him.

John 6:60-65 *Division among the Disciples*

Some of Jesus' followers become scandalized and join the Jews in murmuring and not believing (vv. 60f.). Jesus' reply (vv. 61c-62) employs the familiar Johannine rhetorical device: "If x scandalizes you, then you should see the Son of Man . . . " Here, the greater thing to be seen is Jesus' return to the Father. The sentence functions as a pronouncement of judgment against those who do not believe. John has combined allusions to two types of "Son of Man": those which refer to the coming of the Son of Man as judge (e.g., Mk 14:62) and those which predict his passion (e.g., Mk 10:32ff.). Verse 63 alludes back to the "wisdom" interpretation of the bread when it proclaims that the words of Jesus are spirit and life.

The recapitulation (vv. 64bf.) alludes to the coming betrayal and crucifixion. John wishes to emphasize the fact that Jesus knew that not everyone would believe in him.

He continues to stress the mysterious side of faith by attributing it to the Father. Some interpreters suggest that this story represents a situation in John's community, where people chose to abandon Christianity rather than suffer the penalty of excommunication from the synagogue (cf. the remarks about secret believers in 12:42f.). The Evangelist both warns people against leaving the true salvation and reassures those whose faith may be shaken by such departures.

John 6:66–69 *Peter's Confession*

Scandalized disciples are sharply contrasted with the twelve in this next story. The synoptic story of Peter's confession centers on Jesus' true identity—revealed to the disciples and unknown to the crowd. This story, too, concludes with a Christological identification of Jesus, "God's holy one" (v. 69), but the focus of attention has shifted from that issue to apostasy. Jesus' true disciples realize that he is the one with the words of eternal life. They cannot go to someone else for salvation (an allusion to Moses?).

John 6:70–71 *Passion Prediction*

As in the synoptics, Peter's confession is followed by a prediction of the passion and the statement that one of the disciples is a devil. (In Mk, Peter is called a devil when he tries to dissuade Jesus from the passion.) The Evangelist highlights the fact that one of the twelve will turn and betray Jesus. He may have wished to warn his readers that anyone who turned away from Christianity to another religion was as much a betrayer of Jesus as Judas.

The Success of Jesus' Mission

The Evangelist has reworked traditional materials about the life of Jesus into a rich narrative full of symbolic allusions. At the same time, he has introduced us to the scandal and perplexities that Jesus' ministry and, later, the preaching of the Church caused. On the one hand, he is the definitive revelation of the Father. He can pronounce the divine name, I AM. He is the true bread of life, that is, salvation, for the world. On the other hand, he seems singularly unable to persuade his opponents. The apologetic effort in this chapter seems directed toward believers. Several crises of belief dominate the narrative.

First, there is the question of Jesus as miracleworker. Many Christians talk as though the benefits conferred by belief should convert people to Jesus. Yet in the last chapter, and even more clearly in this one, those who witness Jesus' miracles still disbelieve. The kind of material proof demanded by the crowd cannot be provided. Thus we should beware of the kind of preaching which stresses some physical or mental benefit that is to be gained from our religion.

Second, there is the question of how we are to understand the relationship between Jesus and the messianic expectations of Judaism. Christians sometimes speak of Jesus' fulfillment of the OT in such a way as to make it seem that Judaism, after Christ, is only an anachronism; everything positive has been taken up by Christianity. But John shows clearly that it is possible to accept Jesus as the fulfillment of the OT only if one first accepts him as the one sent from God. Then, his word and ministry become guides for the interpretation of those earlier expectations. Just as miracles cannot produce faith by demonstrating Jesus' authority, detailed exegesis of the OT cannot prove that Jesus is the Messiah to someone without faith.

Third, because he realizes that there is no compelling argument for faith, the Evangelist stresses that it is a gift from the Father. Even Jesus cannot create belief in people. He can only receive those who are given him by the Father (v. 44). At the same time, the gift character of faith does not mean—unlike the conclusion drawn in some Gnostic systems—that those who do not respond are ontologically unable to do so. Although John does not have a systematic explanation of why some believe and others do not, he insists that the nonbeliever will be held responsible for his or her nonbelief. Such a position follows from the gospel's clear assertion that Jesus is the only salvation. He is the only one who has seen the Father. No other religious leader can make such a claim.

Further, the twofold teaching on the bread of life shows that a person must not only believe in the word of Jesus; he or she must also join the community of those who believe. Again, the language of this gospel is not as individualistic as it is sometimes taken to be. Since John insists that miracles are not to be taken literally, we may be sure that he does not have a miraculous understanding of the Eucharist either. It is not some sort of wonder drug which gives eternal life. Rather, the Evangelist is telling us that the kind of secret believers who are mentioned in 12:42 will not "make it." A person must join the community of those who believe. This means that he or she must publicly acknowledge that he or she believes in Jesus as the source of salvation. The discipleship stories earlier in the gospel pointed out another side of that acknowledgment: A person must bear testimony to Jesus.

Neither of these views is particularly congenial to people today. One frequently meets those who claim to be Christians because they like Jesus' teaching, but have no interest in the Christian Church and would not publicly admit to any belief in Jesus. Even among those who attend our churches there is often an uneasy feeling that this really does not matter much. They define Christianity solely in terms of private ethical praxis and often agree with the view that it does not make any difference what a person believes. John does not provide any explanation of Jesus' presence in the Eucharist— though verse 52 makes it clear that those who take Jesus' words literally find them absurd. But he is clear about the fact that a person must belong publicly to the community of believers.

Finally, the whole narrative confronts the reader with the "success question." References to the passion are implied in the statement about Jesus' return to the Father—almost as if to say: If you don't believe that this person is the Messiah now, you never will believe when you hear about the crucifixion—and in the predictions of betrayal. Not only does the crowd fail to understand, but even some disciples withdraw.

Today we hear people—including a Korean "evangelist" who claims to be initiating the messianic age—assert that Jesus failed in his mission. Christian apologists have a tendency to counter such assertions with statistics about converts and church membership—or an appeal to the fact that Christianity grew into a world religion from small beginnings (an argument that could as well prove the divinity of Islam or Buddhism!). John has no such statistics to offer; he must regard faith purely as a gift of the Father. Peter voices the only response the believer can make: He has come to believe that Jesus is the Holy One of God. He alone has the words of eternal life.

7. The Prophet-Messiah from Heaven

The rest of the action takes place in Judea, as the authorities begin to bring formal legal charges against Jesus. The trial and crucifixion of Jesus will conclude the series of legal actions.

A False Prophet?

The formal charge against Jesus in this chapter is that he is a false prophet, for which Jewish law prescribed death by stoning (Dt 18:18–22; B Talmud San 11.5). False prophets were commonly said to lead people astray and to use magic in performing miracles. In the second century, Jews made such charges about Jesus. Justin (*Dial* 69) reports that they called him a deceiver of the people and a magician. The Talmud says that he was executed for leading people astray (B Talmud San 43a, 107b). We also know that false prophets were a problem in the NT period, and the Essene sect opposed someone it called the "man of lies"; many interpreters think that he led members of the sect astray (I Qp Hab 2:2, 5:9–12; CD 20:15). The NT warns Christians against being led astray by false prophets (Mk 13:22 parr, Rv 13:1ff., 19:20). But the accounts of Jesus' trial do not reflect the false-prophet charge, so it was probably not the original charge against him. The Talmudic account of Jesus' death may have been formulated after Jews had encountered Christian preaching. This chapter may take up Jewish charges that were formulated in John's day. It ends with a quasi-legal proceeding against Jesus and includes an attempt to stone him.

In John, the death of Jesus is not some hastily taken decision, precipitated by the events at the Passover. Chapter 7 is set during the fall Festival of Tabernacles, and Jesus' death will not occur until the following spring. The accusation that Jesus is a blasphemer (in ch. 5) occurs in chapter 6, at an unnamed feast prior to the Passover. One year before (in ch. 2), Jesus roused the ire of the authorities by his critique of the temple. Thus the official hostility against Jesus stretches over the whole period of Jesus' ministry.

While we might tend to condemn the Jewish officials for being overly concerned with proving Jesus a false prophet, we should not forget that similar problems confront *us*. People—especially the young—are being lured into all sorts of quasi-religious groups, cults, and movements. Many such groups take advantage of people's legitimate desire for a solution to life's perplexities and their natural feeling that there must be more than what they perceive in their everyday lives. Religious authorities have done little to help them sort out the valuable from the "ripoff" or the perverted; yet almost every week one news medium or another runs a story or expose of some such group. Most of these reports are hampered by the reporters' obvious lack of knowledge about religion.

Early Christians had rules for weeding out false prophets and false missionaries; for example, if a person was becoming rich from preaching the gospel, he was to be rejected. (We may also reject any group which teaches hatred or employs totalitarian tactics.) Nor could a Christian seriously entertain claims that Christ's work is imperfect and requires a further revelation or messiah. Further, as we shall see later in John, Christianity did not isolate people from their society and culture.

If we consider the Jews overly captious, we should see that we do not err in the opposite direction. Concern not to "discriminate" against another group leaves people without the guidelines they have a right to expect. John does not deny the right of officials to question Jesus, but argues that they should have come to a different conclusion.

John 7:1-13 *Jesus' "Brothers" Misunderstand*

The synoptic tradition also preserves the tradition that Jesus' relatives did not understand him (cf. Mk 3:21, 31f., 6:4). Here a false understanding of miracles causes Jesus' "brothers" to suggest that if he goes to a large feast at Jerusalem and does the things he has been doing—some commentators think the Evangelist means the messianic signs—people will believe. Typically in Johannine narrative, Jesus refuses the request at first, and then complies on his own terms. He points out that his time (cp. "hour" in 2:4), the passion, has not yet come.

Verse 1 equates the Jews who are hostile to Jesus with the "world." That equation shows that he does not consider the world a place ontologically hostile to man, as the Gnostics did. When he uses "world" in a negative sense, he is thinking of people who do not believe in Jesus.

Jesus complies with the suggestion on his own terms. He does not go openly. As in the previous chapter, the crowd murmurs, as the Israelites did in the desert (v. 12). Though some decide Jesus is "good," their belief is overshadowed by the formal charge that Jesus is a false prophet. The Evangelist has introduced the motif of the passion and has intensified the mood of hostility. People are now afraid to speak openly about Jesus because of the Jewish authorities. Believers, perplexed by the hostility they encounter, learn from this story that they cannot expect some miraculous activity by God's to turn everyone into a believer. Jesus himself rejects this. People become hostile for a variety of reasons: Some cannot tolerate testimony to their evil deeds; others refuse to discuss or accept Jesus out of fear, rather than malice and ill will.

John 7:14–24 *Jesus Defends his Authority*

The debate about Sabbath healing from 5:18ff. is resumed rather abruptly. The suggestion that Jesus is possessed parallels the charge in Mk 3. The implication that Jesus' lack of education made him unqualified to teach is also found in Mk (1:22, 6:2), where the specific charge is that he had not studied the Scripture, as a rabbi had to do. Similar accusations may have been brought against Christian missionaries. Again, Jesus appeals to his status as the one sent by the Father. He derives everything he says from God; any honor he has, he deserves because he is God's agent. Those who are so concerned to keep the law about killing false prophets are violating it by seeking to kill the true prophet.

The second argument proceeds on humanitarian grounds—like the Sabbath controversies in the synoptics. Jesus previously defended his action on the basis of his right to act as the Father does (5:21ff.); he now uses an acceptable mode of legal reasoning, from the lesser case to the greater. The lesser case is the practice of circumcising children on the Sabbath so as not to break the law. The greater case, healing a person who has been ill for a long time. Verse 22b even dissociates circumcision from the law by claiming that it is only a patriarchal custom. (Perhaps John's church used such an argument to explain why Christians were not required to be circumcised.) Jesus has done more than circumcise; he has healed a whole man.

John 7:25–30 *Is This the Messiah?*

Though the people are amazed by Jesus' knowledge, they

reject him because they think they know his origins (cp. 6:42). The crowd points to the expectation that the Messiah would be hidden on earth until he was pointed out and anointed by Elijah *redivivus*. Since they think they know where Jesus is from, the crowd will not accept him. Jesus' response repeats the assertion that he is from above, from the Father—an origin they do not recognize. That claim divides the crowd, and some make an unsuccessful attempt to seize him. John consistently points out that no one can act against Jesus before the appointed time, and more unsuccessful attempts against Jesus occur in the gospel. The cumulative effect of such incidents is to persuade the reader that the successful attempt against Jesus, the crucifixion, cannot have been an irrational act of violence but must have been a positive part of the work Jesus had been sent to carry out.

John 7:31–36 *Jesus Will Depart*

Verse 31 introduces official reaction to the discussion about Jesus by the crowd. Some are said to believe in Jesus because of his signs (v. 32). The reader knows that such belief cannot be considered reliable. The officials send police to seize Jesus. John continues to stress the fact that Jesus' destiny is under his own control, not the officials'.

Then he introduces a new motif that will dominate the rest of the narrative: Jesus' departure is imminent. The expression "only a little while longer" (v. 33) echoes throughout the farewell discourses (12:35, 13:33, 14:19, 16:16). At the same time, Jesus' departure will be a condemnation of nonbelievers, who cannot follow him (v. 34), in contrast to believers, who will (13:33, 36). Some commentators think that this passage echoes OT descriptions of wisdom, such as that in Prv 1:28f. The people seek wisdom but cannot find it because they do not honor God. Here, the people will look for Jesus but be unable to find him because they do not honor his Father. On the literal level, the people cannot deduce what Jesus is referring to. They think that he means to preach among the Jews who live in the diaspora, and even that misunderstanding has truth in it: by John's time Christianity had spread in just such cities (cp. Jn 17:20).

John 7:37-52 *Questioning Continues*

The second half of the chapter repeats the pattern of the first. Jesus teaches; the people are divided; the officials take action but cannot yet arrest Jesus. John places these events on the seventh day of the feast when the priests carried water from the fount at Gibeon up the temple hill and poured it on the altar. Such a liturgical setting fits Jesus' discourse on living water.

Living Water

Jesus promised living water in 4:10, 14. Water was frequently a symbol of the spirit (Is 49:3, Ez 26:28), and the OT speaks of drinking the wisdom of God (Sir 24:19, 51:23), but verse 38 is ambiguous. It is not clear what passage of Scripture the Evangelist has in mind. Does the passage refer to the believer or to Jesus? If the former, one might think of those passages in which God is said to put the law (= water) into the mouth of the believer (Prv 18:4, Is 58:11, Sir 24:28-33). If the latter, Jesus might be compared to the rock of the Exodus story (Ps 78:15f.). 1 Cor 10:4 provides evidence that such an interpretation of the Exodus story was associated with the Eucharist. The parenthetical addition in verse 39 clearly interprets the saying to describe Jesus' gift of the spirit to the believer.

The Origin of the Prophet-Messiah

Belief that a prophet like Moses would provide living water is part of the same typology as the manna in the previous chapter (Mid Rab Eccles 1:9). Jesus' claim that he provides living water leads some to assume that he is the expected prophet. But once again (cp. 6:42) Jesus' origins—as the crowd understands them—disqualify him: The Messiah is not to be a Galilean. Such arguments may have been frequently used in Jewish–Christian debates. John consistently portrays Galilee as Jesus' earthly home and does not seem to have known the apologetic argument about his birth in Bethlehem, found in Matthew and Luke. Besides, John would not engage in such a debate about earthly origin. For him, Jesus' true origin is heavenly, from the Father.

Authorities Investigate

A quasi-legal investigation follows the return of the temple guards. This scene summarizes the various charges that have been brought against Jesus in the chapter: he leads people astray (v. 47). No one who really knows God's revelation in the OT could accept Jesus; only ignorant crowds follow him (v. 49; cp. 9:34). Nicodemus—a quasibeliever in Chapter 3, where he is presented as a teacher of Israel—intervenes with a legal point that Jesus cannot be condemned without a hearing (Mid Rab Ex 21:3). He is answered with a veiled accusation that he is a disciple of Jesus. The assertion that the prophet cannot be from Galilee is repeated. (One of the earliest manuscripts has *the* prophet in this verse [cp.

v. 40]; others have *a* prophet. The former is more likely correct. It fits the context of this chapter as a technical debate over Jesus' claim to be Messiah.)

John 7:53–8:11   *The Woman Taken in Adultery*

This story is not in the earliest manuscripts of John. Some NT manuscripts locate it after Lk 21:38. The language and style of the story fit a synoptic better than a Johannine context. Luke stresses the theme of forgiveness (e.g., Lk 15:11–32), which is illustrated by this story.

Like synoptic controversy stories, a question is posed with the intent of trapping Jesus (cp. Mk 12:13ff.). He avoids these traps, not by siding with one of the alternatives posed by the interrogator but by finding a third response which dissolves the dilemma. Here, the trap lies in the two laws under which the Jew was required to live. The law of Moses prescribed death for such a person, but the Romans would not allow conquered peoples to exercise jurisdiction in capital cases. Some people thought that the Jewish religious law should be obeyed at all costs. Jesus does not take sides; he puts his questioners in a doublebind by forcing them to realize that they can be put into the same category as the woman.

Although this story did not originally belong to the gospel, it seems to preserve an early piece of tradition. Someone may have copied it into his gospel manuscript to prevent its being lost or, perhaps, to provide a story to go with the seemingly unattached discourse which Jesus delivers in the rest of the chapter.

8. The Divine "I AM"

This discourse picks up many themes of the previous chapters. It seems to have been precipitated by the quasi-legal proceedings of the previous episode. Several parallels to those verses occur here (7:27-30, 8:14-20, 7:33b-36, 8:21-22). Chapter 5 ended with the assertion that Moses stands on Jesus' side. Similarly, this chapter will reject the Jews' claim to be descendants of Abraham, who looked forward to Jesus.

Light of the World

The symbol of light, with which the discourse opens, may be tied to the Feast of Tabernacles, as was the symbolism of running water. Lampstands were set up in the court of the women. Also, John has previously associated light and life (1:4f., 3:19ff.).

Every time John uses the light symbol he does so in the context of its opposite, hostility and rejection. In that respect he differs from the OT, where light, that is, the time of peace and salvation, follows the period of darkness and captivity (cf. Is 42:6, 49:6, 51:4). Dualistic use of the symbol, with light and darkness at the same time, was found among the Essenes, who spoke of members of the sect as sons of light and those outside as sons of darkness (cf. I QS 3:7, 4:7f.). However, John's method of individualizing the symbol is different from the Essenes' and closer to what would result if one read Is 42:6 as referring to an individual rather than the whole nation. John frequently takes images from the OT that were applied to the whole people and applies

97

them to Jesus (cp. the vine in ch. 15). So here. The OT metaphor in Is 42:6 speaks of Yahweh's salvation as dawning like a light and Israel as a light to the nations. John has localized that light in Jesus.

In part, this tendency to localize communal religious metaphors typifies the Hellenistic religious milieu. As civic and corporate modes of religious expression weakened, people turned to individualized cults of salvation. For some, this meant returning to primitive religious practices of magic; for others, it meant allegiance to an individual savior figure or to a religious cult that provided them with a direct link to the divine and immortality. Still others turned away from religion and to philosophies which promised direct contact with the divine that was within the mind of each person. Religious cults and philosophical mysticism could use light/darkness symbolism to express the process by which an individual came to awareness of the divine. Thus whether a person came from a Jewish or a pagan background, he or she could understand that Jesus was claiming to bring true revelation.

At the same time, the reader might be surprised that the image of light is not democratized to include the believer. From the Jewish side, one might expect it to be expanded to include the community (cp. Mt 5:14–16). The expression "sons of light," so common in the Qumran scrolls, occurs only once in the Johannine gospel and epistles (Jn 12:36). Thus it is highly unlikely that it was a designation for members of the community. In fact, the expression "sons" is not used of believers—perhaps because it was perceived as a technical term for the relationship between Jesus and God. Instead, the Johannine literature uses "children." From the pagan side, a person might be struck by the fact that John never speaks of the light as internalized in the believer. He is said to walk in it or to have it, in the sense that he can walk in it while others stumble (12:36), but light does not arise within him. The believer is not enlightened or divinized by the possession of a divine spark. For John, the light is only Jesus (and once the Baptist, by analogy, at 5:35). It is never embodied elsewhere, either in the individual or in the community.

His qualification of the light symbol suggests that John uses such language not only to include a variety of religious options but also to exclude certain features of those same phenomena. He could not accept a Gnostic myth that proposed a divine light within the elect, for example. In our own day, he might criticize expressions about an unmediated presence of the divine within the individual—a Christian adaptation of Yoga or Zen techniques, for example.

John 8:13–20 *Jesus Testifies to Himself*

In chapter 5 (vv. 31–39) Jesus defended himself against the charge that he was illegally bearing witness to himself by calling John the Baptist, his ministry, and the Father (through the Scriptures) as witnesses. This time Jesus refuses the terms of the debate. First, his origin allows him to testify about himself (v. 14). Second, the Father, whom his opponents do not recognize, bears witness to him (vv. 16b–18). Verses 15–16 contrast the truth of Jesus' judgment with that being passed by the Pharisees. They remind the reader that this truth is based on the fact that Jesus is the one sent by the Father. Statements that Jesus does not judge (= condemn) but that his presence brings judgment are frequent in the Fourth Gospel (cf. 3:12–19, 12:47f.). This passage on judgment reminds the reader that the hour is coming when Jesus will be judged falsely, "according to appearances" (v. 15).

John 8:21-30 *Jesus' Departure as Condemnation*

Verses 21-22 parallel the announcement of Jesus' departure in 7:33b-36. Both sections cast that announcement as a prophetic condemnation of disbelief. First, Jesus' opponents were told that they would not be able to come where Jesus is going (7:34). Now, they will die in their sin (v. 21). The singular, "sin," suggests that John is thinking of the sin of not believing in Jesus. In both cases, the audience reacts with misunderstanding which expresses a truth they are unaware of. Their earlier supposition that Jesus would go to the diaspora forecast the spread of Christianity there (7:35). Now they suppose that Jesus' mention of death indicates that he will commit suicide. On the literal level, that is a vicious accusation; such a person could not have any share in the life to come: Jesus would die in his sin. The truth of their statement lies in the fact that Jesus will lay down his life willingly. No one can take it from him.

Jesus goes on to stress the necessity of belief (vv. 23-30). The contrast between Jesus and the crowd is reformulated in terms of origins: They are from below; he is from above. Only those who believe in Jesus' heavenly origin will be able to follow him.

John has used above/below contrasts before to introduce solemn pronouncements about Jesus as Son of Man. Chapter 3:11-15 provides a suggestive parallel to this section. Both follow a scene of misunderstanding with a passion prediction which the audience cannot understand, since they fail to understand a more elementary truth about Jesus. This rhetorical pattern clarifies the logic of this section. Many argue that verses 25b-27 are a later—or parenthetical—intrusion into the passage, since the answer to 25a is the passion prediction. We suggest that the Evangelist inserted these verses prior to the passion proclamation (v. 28) as a statement of the simpler things the crowd does not grasp: Jesus has indeed been sent

by God to speak his word to the world. On this interpretation, the awkward expression in 25b must be a question
(contrary to the NAB). Similar questions introduced the
proclamation of the "greater things" in 1:50 and 3:12.
"From the beginning," then, carries the same pejorative
sense of "earthly things" in 3:14. It is explained by verses
26–27.

Verse 28 associates the crucifixion, using the Johannine
"to lift up the Son of Man," with the revelation of Jesus'
divine identity. (Note that this prediction substitutes an active
verb in "you [= the Jews] lift up" for the theological pas-
sive that is usual in passion predictions. Thus the Evangelist
holds the nonbelieving audience directly responsible for the
crucifixion.) The Evangelist is careful to explain that Jesus'
divinity is predicated on the fact that Jesus carries out the
commission given him by the Father. That analogy has been
used in chapter 5 to explain how Jesus could be identified
with the Father without violating the monotheistic faith of
Israel.

The absolute use of the expression I AM in verses 24 and
28 seems to be derived from the divine self-predication in
the OT. The LXX text of Is 43:10f. is especially striking:

You are my witnesses and I am a witness, says the Lord,
    God
    and the servant whom I have chosen,
that you may know and believe
    and understand that I am.
Before me there was no other God
    and after me there will be none.
I am God
    and no one saves except me.

In this passage we find a call to witnesses. Indeed, God
himself acts as a witness (cp. Jn 8:13ff.). The assertion that

John's testimony demands "knowledge and belief" (cp. vv. 24, 28) in the divine name, I AM, means that only God saves. John applies this text to Jesus. The Evangelist has constantly stressed the fact that Jesus, as Son of Man, is the only Revealer and Savior. Now he tells us that the lifting up of the Son of Man on the cross will reveal that he bears the divine name, I AM.

The pronouncement about the Son of Man is double-edged. It is a judgment oracle against those who do not believe (cp. 12:31, 19:11) and a promise of salvation for those who believe in Jesus' divinity (cp. 12:24, 32). The preceding verses have made clear the negative associations of that pronouncement. Its positive associations are found in the many who believe at the conclusion of the scene. Further, the Johannine reader knows that John always uses "know" in the positive, salvific sense that "knowing God" has in the OT.

The "I AM" Predication

Chapter 8 provides striking examples of the use of the absolute expression I AM as the content of belief. In addition to such absolute I AM sayings, Jesus uses a variety of sentences in which "I AM" is followed by a predicate. The frequency of such expressions in the gospel suggests that the author is drawing upon a well known mode of religious discourse.

The I AM in the OT was the divine name pronounced to Moses (Ex 3:14, 20:5). This expression occurs frequently in the LXX of second Isaiah (43:10f., 45:5f, 18, 22, 46:9, 47:10), where I AM refers to the fact that Yahweh alone is God. Both the pagan gods and the wicked are condemned by their failure to recognize his soverignty. Isaiah 43:10f.,

with its legal terminology and its insistence that only Yahweh
saves, lies particularly close to the language of chapter 8.

On the pagan side, the cult of the popular Egyptian goddess Isis included lists of I AM pronouncements in which the
goddess identified herself with all manifestations of divinity
and indicated that she was responsible for the blessings of
culture. For example:

> I am Isis, the mistress of every land,
>   and I was taught by Hermes
>   and with Hermes I devised writing,
> I gave and ordained laws for men,
>   which no one can change.
> I am the eldest daughter of Kronos.
> I am the wife and sister of Osiris . . .

The Isis cult, in a Hellenized form, was popular throughout the Mediterranean. Diodorus of Sicily (2d century B.C.)
reports having read of stele to Isis and Osiris in Aratana
that were inscribed with I-am sayings similar to those found
in Asia Minor (*Biblio. Histor.*, I 27, 3-6). Thus a person in
John's day might well be acquainted with such language
without belonging to the cult.

We also know that the highly syncretistic religious move-
ment, Gnosticism, used both traditions as part of its esoteric
wisdom. Many versions of the Gnostic myth of the origins
of this evil lower world use material from Genesis. The
god of this world is, so to speak, the God of Genesis—
an ignorant, malevolent deity who wishes to keep people
from realizing that their true home and destiny is in the
divine world of light. Usually there comes a point where
he displays his ignorance of the divine world—from which
he was derived through the fall of his mother—by proclaiming
that he alone is god, an arrogant boast that is immediately

repudiated:

> But he was impious in his ignorance, which was in him,
> for he said, "I am God and there is no other God be-
> side me"—for he was ignorant of his strength [i.e.,
> the light he'd received from his mother], the place
> from which he came [CG II 11, 18–23, cp. Is 43:10].

Later in the same work we find what appears to be a
liturgical fragment—other versions of the story lack this
section—in which the female heavenly revealer describes her
descents to awaken man to his true destiny. She calls to
awaken him from his sleep in ignorance:

I am the Pronoia of pure light;
I am the Thought of the virgin spirit,
   the one who raises you to the glorious place [31, 11–14].

The I-am predications identify the speaker as the revealer
from the light world.

Gnostics apparently composed Isis-style aretalogies in which
the heavenly figure identifies herself with a paradoxical list
of attributes. The heavenly "Eve" pronounces the following
aretalogy:

I am part of my mother;
I am the mother.
I am the virgin;
I am the pregnant one.
I am the physician;
I am the consoler of those in labor [= midwife].
My husband begat me,
   and I am his mother,
   and he is my father and lord [CG II 162, 7–12].

Such paradoxical aretalogies demonstrate the superiority of the Gnostic revealer over the contradictions of the universe. Since they are associated with a female, some suggest that they are an attempt to go Isis one better.

The Gnostics, thus, had three types of I-am predication:

1. The monotheistic claim of 2 Isaiah becomes the boast of an arrogant God who does not even know the source of his power. This perversion of the OT occurs only in Gnostic sources.
2. The revealer uses I-am predications to identify herself to those she summons to their true home.
3. The universality of the aretalogy is expanded to include paradox and contradiction to stress the universality of the Gnostic revealer. The paradoxical type is found only in Gnostic sources. The Gnostic evidence shows clearly that a newly emerging religious group could appropriate Jewish and pagan models at different points in the same story.

In contrast to the Gnostic examples, John uses the 2 Is type positively. Nor do his lists of I-am sayings (with predicates) show any of the contradictory and antithetical character of the Gnostic aretalogies. His I-am sayings suggest four models:

1. "I am," followed by a symbolic predicate:
   bread of life [6:35, 41, 48, 51]
   life [8:12; cf. 9:5]
   gate [10:7, 9]
   good shepherd [10:11, 14]
   resurrection and life [11:25]
   way, truth, and life [14:6]
   vine [15:1, 5]

These symbolic predicates may have originated in Christian

liturgical usage (Schnackenburg, II:64ff.). They provide universal symbols through which believers from a variety of backgrounds may relate to the salvation offered by Jesus.

2. "I am," used by Jesus to identify himself (= "It is I"). The context of these sayings suggests an epiphany since a miraculous happening immediately follows his pronouncing the "I am": 6:20, the sea miracle; 185f., 8, the soldiers immediately fall to the ground. The element of Christophany is also suggested by synoptic accounts of the sea miracle (Mk 6:50 and, even more, Mt 14:33). Again, Is 43:11 is suggestive: Yahweh, the only God, is with his people when they pass through the waters.

3. "I am," followed by an explicit or implicit claim to be the Messiah: 4:26 (Messiah); 8:18 (witness, based on Is 43:10?); 8:23, "from above" (John's favorite expression for Jesus' origin). The "I am," followed by a claim to be Messiah, is also found in the synoptic tradition (Mk 13:6, 14:62).

4. "I am," used absolutely as the content of belief about Jesus : 8:24,28,58; 13:19. This type of I-am pronouncement is uniquely Johannine. It seems to be derived from 2 Isaiah, and represents a claim that Jesus is identical with the Father, as John stated in 5:18. In John, that identity is the central reason for hostility against Jesus. It is the culmination of John's Christology and is without parallel in surrounding religious traditions.

Thus the reader of John would recognize the I-am style as a form of religious language associated with the claims of the deity to exclusiveness (2 Is) and universality (2 Is? Isis) or as the self-identification of a heavenly revealer (Gnostic). But, beyond these forms, he would find the claim to the divine I AM by a person who is said to be a living human being—not Yahweh in heaven, a mythical goddess, nor an emanation of higher aeons—fantastic. One would hardly blame him if he went away shaking his head in puzzlement.

John 8:31–59 *Jesus, Greater than Abraham*

The universality suggested by both the symbol of light and the divine I AM extends beyond the "inner" Jewish debates over Jesus as Messiah and prophet, which dominated the previous chapter. These concerns are addressed as Jesus turns to another revered figure of the Jewish tradition, Abraham. Studies of Jewish missionary preaching show that he was thought to be the father of Gentile converts to Judaism, as well as those who were Jews by birth, since the OT calls him the father of many nations. Such missionary preaching stressed the superiority of Jewish monotheism and ethical values over the pagan religions. By the end of the chapter, Jesus will proclaim his superiority to Abraham with the absolute form of the I AM saying: All the true descendants of Abraham will follow Jesus.

First, Jesus encourages those who have just begun to believe in him by promising that if they continue in that belief (expressions about "remaining" with Jesus imply being his disciple [cf. 1:39]), they will know the truth and the truth will make them free. The Johannine concept of truth is religious. It is neither philosophical nor dogmatic, in that it is not concerned with logically demonstrated propostions and arguments but with following the revelation of God.

The exchange on freedom between Jesus and his audience turns on a combination of nationalistic pride—as sons of Abraham and servants of the true God, the Jews claim to be free—and political reality. Politically, the Jews had not been free for centuries. Many expected the Messiah to be a national liberator who would restore the kingdom of David. The combination of "Abraham," "freedom," "slave," "son," and "heir" in this passage is strikingly similar to that used by Paul in Gal 3. While some (Dodd, *Tradition*, pp. 379–82) have tried to reconstruct a parable about the manumission of slaves behind this passage, we think that Paul and John are using a set topic from Jewish-Hellenistic preaching about Abraham and turning it to show the advantage of Christianity. The Jew, son of Abraham—such a preacher would have argued—is free from the slavery of idolatry. John rejects the claim that descent from Abraham entitles one to salvation (cf. also Lk 16:24, Mt 3:7-10, 8:11f.). Here, the claim is that anyone who sins is a slave—Jew or not. Only the Son, Jesus, can free people. The Christian preacher might then draw the analogy with the son in a Roman household who would free favored slaves when he came into his inheritance (a right that had to be curtailed under Augustus).

After the promise that those who stayed with Jesus would be free, the dialogue shifts back to Jesus' argument with the hostile Jews. By not doing Abraham's work (Jewish sources can speak of faith as Abraham's work) and, even worse, seeking to kill the One whom God has sent (Abraham is renowned in Jewish sources for having welcomed those sent by God, namely, the angels who were sent to tell him of the coming birth of his son Isaac), Jesus' opponents prove that they are sinners and hence slaves (vv. 37-40).

In fact, they act so unlike Abraham that they cannot be considered his sons at all (vv. 41-47). The Jews claim that God is their Father (v. 41); throughout the gospel, Jesus has substantiated his claim that God is his Father by appealing to the works that he does end the word the Father has given him to speak (v. 42). If the Jews really were sons of the same Father, God, they would believe in Jesus (v. 43), rather than seek to kill him (v. 46). Instead, they are sons of the Devil (the Essenes used the expression "sons of Beliar" for enemies of the sect [I QS 1:10]), who is a murderer and inspires such deeds in others.

The mention of the Devil as Jesus' real antagonist deepens the mood of hostility that has built up in these chapters. From here on, Jesus is not merely opposing men but must vanquish the Devil as his real antagonist (12:31, 14:30, 16:11, 17:15).

Picking up on the mention of Satan, Jesus' opponents launch a countercharge: he is the one with a demon (v. 48; cp. Mk 3:22–25). The accusation that Jesus was a Samaritan only occurs here; it probably depends on Jewish anti-Samaritan slander and associations between Samaritans and magicians (cp. Acts 8). Jesus' defense is consistent with what he has said throughout: he does not seek his own glory (vv. 50, 54). Such a defense might have been used by anyone accused of magic in antiquity.

But—typical of Johannine discourse—Jesus does not spend much time defending himself. He moves to an even bolder announcement: The believer (= the one who keeps Jesus' word [cf. 14:21–24, 15:20, 17:6]) will never see death. Literal interpretation of Jesus' words leads the crowd to make a true statement which they think would condemn Jesus: He claims to be greater than Abraham and the prophets. John may be using a traditional Christian exegetical tradition that interpreted the rejoicing of Abraham (Gn 17:17; cf. Jub 14:21, 15:17) as rejoicing over seeing Jesus' day (Lk 10:24, Heb 11:13, 1 Pt 1:10ff.). The crowd turns Jesus' words into an absurd literal statement—that such a young man is claiming to have seen the patriarchs. This interpretation leads to the climax of the chapter: "Before Abraham was, I AM" (v. 58).

No clearer claim to divinity could be made—though one

might take the sentence to mean simply that God exists before Abraham. John is not concerned to specify the relationship between Jesus and the Father which makes such pre-existence possible. The crowd understands Jesus to have made a blasphemous claim to equality with God and tries to execute the stroning penalty mandated in the law.

9. The Man Born Blind

The previous chapter opened by describing Jesus as light of the world (8:12). The carefully elaborated miracle story in this chapter demonstrates the symbolic meaning of that theme by contrasting the spiritual blindness of Jesus' opponents with the insight of the believer. This story forms a positive counterpart to the one in chapter 5, where the man did not come to believe in Jesus. Here, the blind man withstands hostility to testify to Jesus and comes finally to worship him. (The story in chapter 5 is the only one where faith does not result from the miracle. It is also the only miracle story in John where the miracle is not given a symbolic interpretation.)

The more the blind man in this story is questioned, the more clearly he speaks about Jesus. The care with which this story has been divided into scenes and the progressive development of the man's faith suggest that this story reflects experiences common in John's day. About A.D. 90, Jews excommunicated Christians from the synagogue, and throughout this story the participants fear such a punishment. Since synagogue communities provided an individual with a religious, social, educational, legal, and even welfare structure, it is easy to see how such a penalty would have been a severe test of faith for Christians who still lived in such communities.

It is difficult to guess how much of the story was traditional, since there are no close parallels in the synoptic stories about Jesus' healing the blind. Perhaps verses 1–3a, 6, and 7 give the outline of the traditional story: Jesus worked the miracle to repudiate a popular belief that all blind or handicapped people deserved it—either they or their parents had sinned.

Although people do not often say so outright, those who work with the handicapped today encounter similar attitudes: Outsiders consider the handicapped bad, almost criminal, while the latter may feel that God is punishing them for some unknown sin. Both feelings are wrong and destructive to the attempts such people make to lead a happy, productive life; but they are very difficult to overcome.

John expands that traditional story to show that this blind man gains more insight into who Jesus is than any of the religious experts who are arrayed against him. Undoubtedly, the story would have encouraged Christians whose faith may have been shaken when the Jewish religious authorities took formal action against them.

Like a true disciple (vv. 8-12), the man openly testifies that Jesus is the one who healed him. (The man in chapter 5 did not know who healed him.) Typically, since Jesus' heavenly origin is a mystery in the gospel, the man cannot say where Jesus is.

The authorities step in to investigate. First, they try to persuade the man that since Jesus worked on the Sabbath, he could not be from God (vv. 13-17). But their questioning only drives the man to a deeper conviction about Jesus—to have worked such a sign he must be a *prophet*.

Then (vv. 18-23) they attack the miracle itself by trying to get the man's parents to say that he was not blind from birth. The parents insist that he was, but refuse to become further involved because they are afraid of being put out of the synagogue.

Finally (vv. 24-34), the authorities intensify their interrogation. First (v. 25), they attempt to use their authority to persuade the man to call Jesus a sinner. When that fails, they accuse the man of being Jesus' disciple rather than a true follower of Moses, whom everyone knows spoke for God—not like Jesus, whose origin is unknown (vv. 28f.). As soon as the question of origin is introduced, the man responds by saying that a person would have to be *from God* in order to do the miracle Jesus has done—and even the Pharisees should be able to figure that out (vv. 30–33). The officials rebuke him as an obvious sinner—because he had been born blind?—who has no right to instruct them. They cast him out of the synagogue.

These hostilities did not separate the man from Jesus and bring him back to Judaism. Instead, he has moved from knowing Jesus' name (v. 11), to calling him a prophet (v. 17), to rejecting the view that Jesus is a sinner to have worked on the Sabbath (v. 25), to declaring that, like Moses, Jesus is from God (v. 33). John wishes to encourage Christians to show similar steadfastness.

The conclusion (vv. 35–41) falls into two parts as Jesus confronts each group to reveal their insight or blindness. So far, the blind man has drawn the one positive conclusion from the evidence, which Jesus has said should be shown by his works: that Jesus is indeed from God. A further meeting with Jesus is necessary. Like the other conversion stories in John, this one has two stages for the man to learn Jesus' full identity: he is the heavenly Son of Man. This expression carries all the connotations of divinity that have been developed in the previous chapters. As soon as the man learns Jesus' identity, he falls down and worships him (v. 38).

But the Johannine Son-of-Man sayings usually carry two edges: promise for the believer and judgment for the nonbeliever. So here. The worship of the believer is followed by a judgment oracle against the Pharisees (v. 39). The blind man has learned Jesus' true identity and worshiped; the religious experts, who claimed to know what God required, are blind to Jesus' origin. All their efforts to keep the law and avoid sin are in vain.

This story must have encouraged Christians, who would

have frequently found themselves in the position of the blind man vis-a-vis the religious establishment. Even for readers who were not concerned with Jewish polemics, it would provide dramatic confirmation of the superiority of Christianity. Even an uneducated blind man could see the truth about Jesus and believe.

10. The True Shepherd of Israel

This discourse on the true shepherd picks up the condemnation of the Pharisees from the last chapter. (In Lk 15:3-7 the parable of the lost sheep is directed against the Pharisees.) The key OT source for this polemic is the shepherd image in Ez 34. God directs the prophet to condemn the shepherds of Israel and promises that he, himself, will seek out, gather from the diaspora, and care for his sheep. That long speech concludes with the proclamation: "And they shall know that I am the Lord, their God, and they are my people. House of Israel, says the Lord, you are my sheep and the sheep of my shepherd and I, the Lord your God, says the Lord" (Ez 34:30f. LXX). John 10 ends with the proclamation that the people will know the identity of Jesus and the Father. The Evangelist has drawn on many of the images in Ez 34 as he puts Jesus in the place of the Lord in Ezekiel's prophecy.

John 10:1-6 *Sheepfold Parables*

Commentators are divided as to whether one or two short parables are contained in these verses. Given John's preference for double stories, he may have created a double parable from the single image of the shepherd by associating the gate (Ps 118:19, of righteousness; 20, of the Lord) with the shepherd. That association may have been instigated by his reflection on the death of Jesus, since Ps 118:18, 22 speaks of the suffering that the righteous person will undergo at the hands of the wicked. These verses helped Christians understand the death and resurrection of Jesus.

115

Verses 1-3a focus on how a person enters the sheepfold as an indication of his relationship to the sheep. Verses 3b-5 focus on how the sheep respond to the true shepherd. As in all parables, it is difficult to determine how far to carry the allegorizing process. Some suggest that the parable alludes to the previous story: Like the blind man, Jesus' sheep will not follow the strange voices of the Pharisees. Verse 6 would then refer to the Pharisees' not understanding that they are the strangers and robbers. But verse 6 could refer to the audience's as a whole not understanding the parable. We favor this latter interpretation because it may have been a literary convention to join a parable with its interpretation by a statement about the audience's misunderstanding (cf. Mk 4:11f.). This convention gives the interpretation the status of a true, hidden, or esoteric teaching for the person with true insight.

John 10:7-21 *Interpretations of the Parables*

Several interpretations of the gate/shepherd image are given, and all are Christological. They will lead to a division of opinion about Jesus.

The first interpretation of Jesus as the gate (vv. 7f.) says that no one can approach the sheep except through Jesus. Anyone else who claimed to bring revelation would be a thief and robber. The sheep should not listen to him.

Turning to the relationship between the sheep and the gate (vv. 9f.), Jesus proclaims that those who pass through him will find pasture—a common metaphor for salvation (cf. Ez 34:12-15). "Have life to the full" (v. 10) clearly designates Jesus as the one who brings the life that is to be characteristic of the new age.

The first interpretation of Jesus as ideal shepherd (vv.

11-13) contrasts his willingness to die for his sheep (v. 11; cp. 15:13) with other leaders, who would abandon them. Verses 14-15 elaborate on the relationship between Jesus and the sheep. Because they know him, that is, remain with him, Jesus' sheep will not be lured away. John 10:28 and 17:12 make it clear that Jesus is referring to the possibility that hostility and counterargument will cause some to lose their faith in him. Lest such losses cause others to doubt, he assures his listeners that none of those for whom he is about to die will be lost (v. 15). The relationship between Jesus and his own is compared to that between himself and the Father. That new relationship will be a major theme of the last discourses and part of his legacy to the Church.

Verse 16 reminds the reader that Jesus' flock will not be limited to Jews, the renewed Israel. John has stressed the universal scope of Jesus' mission from the beginning. Jesus' death will bring into being a new community of Jew and Gentile (11:52, 12:20-23, 17:20-24).

Understanding the Death of Jesus

Some might find the death of Jesus a direct contradiction of his claim to intimate association with God and to divine protection for his flock. (After all, if the wolf eats the shepherd, he can have the whole flock!) Therefore, throughout the passion narrative, John emphasizes the voluntary nature of Jesus' death (vv. 17f.). His death does not mean that Jesus failed to do God's will and was punished. It does not break the close association between Jesus and his Father.

Although the OT often pictures premature death as a divine punishment, the persecution of righteous Jews in the two centuries before Christ had led many to new understandings of righteousness and persecution. Wisdom 5 contains a dramatic scene in which the wicked plot to put a righteous man to a shameful end as a test of his faithfulness to God and of God's love for him. They think that by killing the righteous man they demonstrate that God does not care about him. But the judgment brings a rude surprise. The man they persecuted is exalted into heavenly glory and numbered among the angels.

Christians frequently turned to this scene to describe the death/exaltation of Jesus. Only a righteous person who died willingly, out of love for God and his law, could expect such exaltation. The controversy stories have shown Jesus' opponents trying to convince people that not only could Jesus not have been the Messiah, because he did not fulfill the messianic prophecies, but he could not have been a righteous person, since he broke the law by blasphemously claiming identity with the Father and by healing on the Sabbath. The Evangelist stresses the fact that the Father loves Jesus precisely because he *did* lay down his life, in obedience to him command (v. 18). Jesus *did* die "beloved of God," and is exalted in heaven.

Division among the People

Jesus' words lead to division of opinion (vv. 19-21). Some conclude that he is mad (cp. 7:20, 8:48, 52), the frequency of the charge suggests that is may have been standard anti-Christian polemic. Others take a positive view of his words and the healing of the blind man. (Here the shepherd gives life; in ch. 9, light. The two symbols are closely associated in Jn 1:4.) The miracle in chapter 9 ended with a strong condemnation of the Pharisees and their attempts to instruct the blind man in the law of Moses. Jesus' remarks here also seem to be directed against them. They are the ones who came before Jesus, as they themselves might well have pointed out; their oral traditions were said to go back to Moses on Sinai. How could Christians claim such authority for Jesus? Thus we do not agree with those who see the references to hired hands (v. 8) or those who came before Jesus (v. 12) as allusions to messianic pretenders. John gives no evidence that they were a problem in his community (unlike Mk 13:6, 22 and Mt 7:15, note the wolves in sheep's clothing).

The True Religious Leader

In contrast to the Pharisees, Jesus provides a striking model for any religious leader. (Greek works often describe the ideal king as shepherd of his people.) Such a person must be devoted to the welfare of others. He or she cannot be subject to the suspicion that he or she is satisfying his or her greed or psychological ego needs at the expense of his or her followers. We are very skeptical of people in leadership positions, since they frequently fail to convey the attitude of care and concern that Jesus epitomizes in the image of the shepherd. But our skepticism is not a new, twentieth-century invention; the prophetic condemnation of the leaders of Israel in Ez 34 is as strong as anything we might say.

Ezekiel's answer is to point to God as the true shepherd of Israel. John sees those promises fulfilled in Jesus. Both suggest that the model of leadership they promise can only be grounded in the nature of God himself. It is God's compassion for his people that is manifested in such leaders. People who claim to be leaders but act on the basis of their desire for glory or office will never convince us that they would lay down their lives for those under them.

John 10:22-42 *Jesus and the Father Are One*

Although John sets this discussion at a later time—to extend the period of Jesus' ministry in Jerusalem—it takes up from the previous one. Jesus had claimed to be the eschatological shepherd of Israel, and now the crowd asks to be told plainly whether or not he is the Messiah (v. 24). The reader knows by now that Jesus *does* claim to be the Messiah, though not always in the terms people expect. Jesus' answer says as much. Anyone who has seen his "works" (a comprehensive term for his whole ministry) would know that he is (v. 25).

Disbelief is then explained by saying that some people do not belong to his fold. Although such statements are sometimes read to imply a dualistic division of humanity into those destined to believe and those not so predestined, it need not mean anything more in this context than that those who are questioning Jesus obviously do not believe anything he has said. They will not accept him as Messiah, no matter what he does or says. The emphasis falls on the second part of Jesus' statement: None of his sheep will be lost (vv. 28b-29). The function of this section is not to provide a systematic account of Jewish disbelief but to reassure the believer, in the face of that disbelief, that he or she is right. No one and no argument can separate him or her from Jesus; God will see to that.

As so often happens in John, the discourse then moves beyond discussion of Jesus as Messiah to a broader assertion that Jesus is one with the Father (v. 30). An attempt is made to execute the legal penalty for blasphemy: Stoning (v. 31; cp. 8:59. Mark 14:64 parr. give blasphemy as the Jewish charge against Jesus.). The charge that Christian belief in the divinity of Jesus is blasphemous has been raised frequently in the gospel (cf. 5:18f.; cp. 19:4). The reader has already learned that the answer to such accusations is to point out that, as agent of the Father, Jesus may be considered identical with the One who sent him. That identity depends on the fact that Jesus is only in the world to do what the Father has sent him for. The conclusion (vv. 37f.) makes that point. It informs the whole presentation of Jesus in this gospel: He is the one sent by God; all his works are from God; everything has been handed over to him by the Father.

The first answer Jesus gives in this section employs a more typically Jewish mode of argument, however, and may represent another line of defense taken by the Johannine Church. A biblical passage (Ps 82:6) is quoted in which single Israelites are called "gods" and warned that they will die like men. (The judgment context of this passage, predicting death for the wicked, may be intended as a counterimage to the life Jesus gives his sheep [v. 28].) Rules of argument allowed a person to proceed from a lesser case, that is, sinful Israelites, to a greater—one sent by God. If the term gods can apply in the lesser case, it may also be used in the greater, Jesus.

The final verses (40–42) form a positive conclusion to the Jerusalem ministry—a negative conclusion will follow in chapter 12. It brings the reader back to the testimony of the Baptist: Everything that he said about Jesus has been demonstrated. No matter how negative a picture he paints, John does not want his readers to lose sight of the fact that people believed in Jesus despite all the hostility and counterargument (cf. 11:45, 12:9, 17–19).

Despite his equality with God, Jesus will lay down his life for the sheep. While many early Christian hymns (e.g., Phil 2:5–11) speak of the contrast between Jesus' divinity and his earthly life as one of humiliation, John never uses such language. Jesus' death for his sheep is not a humiliation but the epitome of God's concern for his people, as that concern was portrayed in the shepherd image.

There have been modern-day arguments that all social volunteer work is degrading, since it deprives people of the status and pay their talents deserve. Further, it leads to an unwillingness by society to pay for needed social services if people think that volunteers can do all such jobs. Christians should not fall victim to such arguments or to a language which suggests that service to others is inferior to high-paying or high-status employment. Otherwise, they may carry that attitude over to their relationship with Jesus. Even though he is Son of God, he may be felt to be inferior to the wise and powerful of the world and his teaching a secondary concern in the formulation of one's priorities in life.

11. The Resurrection and the Life

This chapter exploits the life/death contrast in the gospel by making the raising of Lazarus the cause of Jesus' death (11:46-53; cf. 12:9-11). John has probably reworked a traditional miracle, such as we find in the synoptics (Mk 5:22f.; cf. Mt 11:5). The following verses are usually attributed to his source: 1, 3, 5, 33-34, 38-39a, 41a, 43a, and 44. Since the dialogues between Jesus and each sister are similar, commentators suggest that the original story may have had one exchange between Jesus and unnamed sisters or between Jesus and Martha, which was then elaborated with the addition of one of the famous women of Christian tradition, Mary. Jesus' apparent refusal (vv. 4, 6) to respond to the request—even for someone he loves (a symbol of the relationship between Jesus and the Christian?)—is typical of the Johannine miracle story. As usual, he is far less interested in the miracle itself than in the symbolic significance of the deed: Jesus is the resurrection and the life. Verse 4 introduces the symbolic level of what is to occur (cp. 9:3). The irony of Jesus' statement is increased by the fact that the reader realizes that the glorification of the Son begins with his death (12:23f.).

John 11:7-16 *Jesus Turns to Go to Judea*

John immediately ties the miracle to the impending passion by introducing this dialogue between Jesus and his disciples over the dangers of returning to Judea. (Contrast 7:1ff., where Jesus refused to go to Judea because it was not time for him to die.) The scene makes is clear once again (cp. Lk 9:51) that Jesus chooses what happens to him. He is not the victim of some accidental fate that he would avoid if he could. The disciples are equally aware of the dangers that await them but decide to go with him (v. 16). What they do not yet understand is that Jesus' death is for the glory of God. They still perceive it as something to be avoided, if at all possible.

On the human level, we find the same phenomenon with twentieth-century martyrs, such as Gandhi, Martin Luther King, and even Malcolm X. Before their assassination, each had reached a state of identification with his mission so that personal danger and death were not important. Each predicted that he would meet a violent death and each had followers who tried to dissuade him from going to the city, rally, or demonstration where he met his death. For some of them, Jesus' fate was an important model. Jesus does not simply ignore his disciples' fear (cp. Mk 10:32-34). He tries to use the raising of a dead person to show them that death is not the end of life. His own death will not invalidate his mission. Therefore, their faith should not be shaken by his death—symbolized in the story by the death of someone he loved (vv. 14f.).

John 11:17-27 *Jesus, the Resurrection and the Life*

Jesus arrives after Lazarus has been dead four days. Rabbinic opinion held that the soul remained near the body for three days, after which there would be no hope of a person's reviving. Martha expresses her conviction that God listens to Jesus and that, had Jesus been there, her brother would not have died. That belief is still linked to Jesus' miracle-working ability. She does not understand the true significance of Jesus' gift of life. Unlike the earlier miracles, the dialogue that explains the significance of the miracle occurs before the event. That change may be due to the fact that John's source had some dialogue at this point.

Jesus begins with a statement that fits the general eschatological expectations of Judaism. Does Martha believe in the resurrection? Jesus seems to have agreed with the Pharisees, against the Sadducees, in holding that belief. Daniel 12:1-3 is the only OT witness to the doctrine. Belief in the resurrection apparently arose during the Seleucid persecution of the Jews as an explanation of the fate of those righteous Jews who died rather than renounce their faith. Thus, in a popular story about seven martyred brothers, one says: "One cannot but choose to die at the hands of men and to cherish the hope that God gives of being raised by him. But for you [= the persecutors] there will be no resurrection of the dead" (2 Mc 7:14). The general belief in the resurrection, then, implied a positive reward of life for the pious Jew. The wicked could expect nothing except death; even if they are resurrected, as in Daniel, it is for eternal punishment. They will not share in the life of the glorious new age.

After Martha says that she holds this general belief in the resurrection, Jesus claims that he is the resurrection and the life. Being a pious Jew will not be enough to gain the expected reward; a person must also believe in Jesus. Martha responds with a confession of faith: Jesus is Messiah, Son of God, the one sent by him.

John 11:28-37 *Jesus and Mary*

The opening of this scene reminds us of the paired discipleship stories of chapter 1. A person responds to faith in Jesus by summoning another. Martha's summons to Mary provides an audience to witness the miracle, and Mary

voices the same objection her sister had (v. 32). This time
no theological answer to the problem of the death of the
believer is given. Instead, the following verses bring the
same question to the lips of the crowd by making it clear
that Jesus loved Lazarus, that is, that Lazarus was a true
disciple of Jesus (cp. 16:27). The reader has already been
instructed that anyone whom Jesus loves has life and that
he or she should not suppose that physical death destroys
that life.

John 11—38-44 *Lazarus Raised*

Martha's objection to removing the stone shows that despite her profession of faith, she does not have confidence
in his word. The promise that what is about to happen
will show the glory of God recalls other miracles (2:11, 9:3).
The expression "to see the glory of God" also has a natural
association with resurrection language: the glory of God is
revealed to the nations in the last days. The reader knows
that Jesus is the one in and through whom the glory of
God is seen.

Jesus' prayer (vv. 41f.) may be from the traditional account. Miracles in rabbinic sources stress the role of prayer.
Prayer makes it clear that the rabbi does not act on his
own power, like a magician, but is dependent upon God.
The Evangelist has expanded the prayer motif (v. 42) to
make it clear that the relationship between Jesus and God
is unique. People may be confident that God answers Jesus'
prayer (vv. 21, 37), but they still need to understand the
true relationship between Jesus and his Father. Johannine
prayers typically express the unity between the two (v. 42c;
cp. 17:20f.).

Jesus Overcomes Death

Parallels between this story and the piece of traditional eschatology in Jn 5:28-29 make this story a vivid illustration of that teaching. Jesus is the one who summons the righteous to resurrection:

Do not be amazed at this, the hour is coming when all those in the tombs [*like Lazarus*] will hear his [= Son of Man] voice [*Jesus shouts in a loud voice,* v. 43]. And will come out [*Lazarus is summoned to come out,* v. 43]. Those who have done good to *resurrection of life* [*resurrection and life,* v. 25].

These parallels demonstrate the real meaning of the story. As usual, John shows little interest in the literal details.

Such a clear demonstration that Jesus is the one who summons the righteous to judgment should make it clear to the believer that the death of Jesus does not vindicate the position of his opponents that Jesus was a sinner, madman, and false prophet, who led people away from God's revelation in the Torah.

Many Christians today find it difficult to face either their own death or that of someone close to them. We even find that art in newer churches uses the motif of Jesus' exaltation on the cross to portray an ascending or risen Christ, rather than a dead one. Such artistic developments can be helpful if they remind Christians that Jesus has triumphed over death, but they can play into our contemporary neuroses if they are a way of avoiding the fact that all must pass through death. Many of us have a hard time allowing people to die, just as Lazarus' sisters and friends thought that the only way Jesus could show his love for his friend was to cure him. We badly miss the point of the story if we take it to mean that Jesus agrees with them and finally gets around to doing what he should have done all along. The dialogue with Martha made it clear at the beginning that Jesus did not come to "make up" for his earlier neglect of their request; he wishes to demonstrate the basis for Christian confidence that death is not the end. A Christian's life goes beyond death, and will be more glorious than this one. A person with such confidence in God's life-giving power can allow himself, herself, and others to die in peace whenever the in time comes. A person who feels that once he or she dies, there is nothing, cannot allow that. Such a person would hardly choose to die as Jesus is about to do, from his sense of the mission God has given him.

Many people say they cannot believe in life beyond death because they cannot believe in angels with wings (not biblical angels!), harps, and gold streets. But notice that none of the passages we have cited from the Bible commit a person to believe in such a scenario. The Bible uses a variety of images to express confidence not only that life continues but that it has certain characteristics:

1. It is in some sense individual; a person does not merge into some great stream of life or energy.
2. Its quality is a function of a person's belief or disbelief and actions in this life.
3. It is not like, or a repeat of, this life. (Despite many attempts to demonstrate the contrary, no biblical author teaches a doctrine of reincarnation. The notion that God intended to return Elijah to earth at the end-time is not evidence for such a belief. When the doctrine makes an appearance in Christian authors it is derived from Platonic philosophy.)
4. The righteous will be truly happy and will attain the vision of God which they sought in this life.

No one can prove that such a life exists. The Jews who believed in it in Jesus' day expected it to come with the end of the world. Christians believe that Jesus has already passed through death into that resurrected life and thus assures us of a similar destiny.

John 11:45-57 *Authorities Act Against Jesus*

The Lazarus miracle, too, provokes division and formal juridical action by the authorities. There are some hints in the synoptic tradition that an earlier meeting of officials may have led to the decision to arrest Jesus (cf. Mk 14:1-2, Mt 26:1-5, Lk 22:1-2), but it is difficult to assess the historical accuracy of the tradition at this point. Verses 49 and 51 speak of Caiaphas as high priest that year—in fact, the office was held for an indefinite period. Caiaphas was high priest until shortly after Pilate was removed from office in A.D. 36, a coincidence that has led some historians to suppose that he may have held the office through some financial arrangement with Pilate; the office was frequently bought in this period. (John 18:13 wrongly designates Annas high priest.)

The Evangelist makes the most of the "testimony" the characters give to Jesus. Ability to prophesy was associated with other high priests (cf. Jos., *Ant* XI. viii. 4; XIII. x. 7). Typical of Johannine irony, the speakers think they are talking about political problems, but speak the truth on another level. They are afraid that Jesus will be the sort of political messiah who will lead a mass revolt, such as resulted in the Romans' destruction of Jerusalem in A.D. 70 (vv. 47f.; cp. Mk 14:57ff.). Their concern that many will believe as a result of Jesus' signs (vv. 47b–48a) will be true on a different level: the whole world (= Gentiles) will follow Jesus.

The Evangelist has underscored the irony of Caiaphas' prediction by having it begin with a reprimand: "You understand nothing" (v. 49c). In spite of his ignorance, Caiaphas makes a true statement. Jesus' death will be *for the people,* but it will not avert the political catastrophe the leaders fear. Language about Jesus' death *for the people,* may be drawn from the eucharistic formula of the Johannine Church (cf. 6:51c), where the death of Jesus is given a different ecclesiological turn: It will bring Jews and Gentiles into one, new people of God (vv. 51b–52; cp. 12:32. A similar view of the reconciling effect of Jesus' death is found in the hymnic material in Eph 2:11–15.). From that perspective, the political divisions at the basis of the proceedings in this chapter are meaningless. Jesus' death will draw the Gentiles to him (12:32). They too are children of God. The chosen people will no longer be defined by ethnic descent and national boundaries. The hearing closes with a formal sentence of death (v. 53).

John concludes the chapter with the theme of the withdrawal and mysteriousness of Jesus' movements (cp. 7:1–13). While people are wondering if Jesus will appear, the reader is reminded that "a contract is out on him" (v. 57).

12. The Hour Begins

This chapter includes events that the synoptic tradition associates with the passion, and the discourse material ties those events to specifically Johannine themes. This is the last time in the gospel that Jesus speaks to the "world." Rejection of his word turns it to one of judgment.

John 12:1-8 *Anointing at Bethany*

The synoptic tradition has two anointing stories: one during the public ministry at the house of a Pharisee (Lk 7:36-50), the other, as here, in Bethany before the Passover (Mk 14:3-9, Mt 26:6-13). John's version shares details with both stories. He links the story to the previous chapter by having it occur in the house of Lazarus (Luke has Simon, the Pharisee; Mt/Mk have Simon, the leper). He probably had a version of the story which did not indicate whose house was involved. In Mk 14:4f., some of the disciples are angry about the waste of such valuable ointment; they argue that the sale price could have been given to the poor. Here the motif of the anger of the disciples has been transferred to Judas. His objection provides the Evangelist with an opportunity to comment on his character—he is a thief (v. 6; cp. Mt 26:15, greed).

It has always been difficult for Christians to understand how someone who has been closely associated with Jesus could have betrayed him. This story provides one explanation; Jn 6:70 has already given another: Judas is possessed (cp. 13:2, 27, Lk 22:3). Neither view solves all the problems. Why would Jesus have chosen such a person? Why didn't

131

he heal him? These questions serve to remind us that even though the Johannine Church had such a striking picture of Jesus' divinity that some authors even allege that it had no real concept of his humanity, nevertheless it realized that Jesus was indeed subject to the limitations of life in this world, where evil is a perplexing mystery.

Concern for the Poor

By having Judas voice the objection, John takes some of the edge off Jesus' reply, "Leave her alone. Let her keep it against the day they prepare me for burial. The poor you always have with you, but me you will not always have" (v. 7f.). People sometimes take the expression "the poor you always have with you" out of context and use it to justify a certain skepticism about welfare programs. But that expression was probably a proverb based on Dt 15:11, and when we look at the whole sentence to which it alludes we cannot accept such an interpretation. The OT passage encourages people to take care of the poor; to obey the sabbatical year provisions lest the poor cry out to God against the people. "For the poor will never cease out of the land. Therefore I command you. You shall open wide your hand to your brother, to the needy and to the poor in the land" (Dt 15:11).

It is false to that teaching for a thief to want to sell what the woman has brought and give it to the poor. The Deuteronomic legislation was not concerned with such an individual but with a consistent pattern of action toward the poor, to be applied by the people as a whole. We know from the OT prophets and from Jesus' criticism that often the law was not observed. (One could hardly accuse a person who acts with such generosity toward Jesus of the hard-

hearted abuse of the poor that is condemned in Deuteronomy.) That is where the issue lies—not in fighting over
the expenditure of money for some other purpose. On the
other hand, Deuteronomy takes a more realistic view of the
problem than does the rhetoric of some of our social programs. Poverty will not be removed permanently from the
land. This open-handed generosity will always be called for.
We could even say that those who look for the opposite
betray a secret lack of generosity—a "let's wipe out poverty
so I don't have to give anymore" attitude. Jesus' saying,
then, does not reject the principle of concern for the poor;
he merely rejects the attempt to invoke it against the woman.
She is the first person in the gospel to realize that Jesus'
hour has come.

John 12:9–11 *Action against Lazarus*

John pursues his parallel with Jesus' gift of life as the
cause of his death by inserting reminders of the belief en-
gendered by that miracle. The authorities would like Lazarus
to suffer a fate similar to that planned for Jesus—an allusion to the fate of some later Christian missionaries (v. 9;
cf. 16:2)?

John 12:12–19 *Entry into Jerusalem*

This story is told differently in each gospel. In part, the
variations represent the different understandings each author
has of the event. John reminds us of the Lazarus story by
having the crowd be those who had heard about the miracle
(vv. 17–19). The Pharisees' remark that the world is following Jesus reminds us that the authorities were afraid of this

(11:48). It may also allude to Jesus' remark that he has other sheep (10:16). The true meaning of the scene is understood as a universal acclamation of Jesus' kingship.

Unlike the synoptic versions, there is no search for an animal. Jesus does not ride into the city but only sits on the beast after the first acclamation by the crowd. The reader already knows that Jesus will not fulfill nationalistic hopes for a king (6:14; note the similar language about a sign and one coming into the world). The crowd's acclamation seems to be nationalistic. Palms were a symbol of liberation on the coins of the second revolt, and the Jews carried them at the rededication of the temple (2 Mc 10:7). Further, the expression "go out to meet" is used of crowds when they go to welcome a king. The line that is added to the psalm quote, "you are the king of Israel," heightens the nationalistic implications of the crowd's action.

So far, there has been little discussion of the title "king" in the gospel. The Evangelist saves that for the passion narrative, where it becomes the focus of the trial before Pilate. According to the Evangelist's arrangement of the story, verses 14–15 must provide the clue to the significance of the event. Now that his "hour" has come, Jesus appears to accept an acclamation as king. But we are warned that this action was not really understood until after the resurrection (v. 16). The quotation that is invoked to explain Jesus' action also appears in Matthew, but with the correct "riding" or "mounted," while John has "seated". Perhaps the change represents an assimilation of the passage to the image of Jesus enthroned as king. The "rejoice greatly" of the Zec 9:9 quote seems to have arisen by assimilation to the opening of Zep 3:16. (Matthew 21:5 also changes the opening, from "rejoice, O daughter of Zion" to "tell the daughter of Zion." Matthew stresses the humility mentioned in the passage, which John, who does not use metaphors of humility, omits.) Both OT passages are prophecies of a time when God will come into the midst of his people (in Zephaniah the Lord is king; in Zechariah his messiah is), liberate them from all their enemies, and make them a nation exalted over all others. Jesus, clearly, did not fulfill any of these expectations, but John hints that the conversion of the Gentiles provides the key to the true meaning of this passage.

John 12:20-26 *Greeks Come to Jesus*

The coming of the Greeks (= Gentiles) illustrates the fulfillment of that promise and also signals the arrival of Jesus' hour (v. 23). Jesus responds to their desire to see (= believe in) him by predicting his passion.

The group of sayings in verses 24–26 is from a tradition similar to what we find in the synoptics (cp. Mk 4:32, 8:34ff.). Mark 8:34ff. shows that the last two sayings on discipleship were commonly associated with Jesus' passion.

Interpreters suggest that the saying about the grain of wheat (v. 24) is a miniature parable. Like the mustard seed parable (Mk 4:32), it stresses the point that the yield will be great (cp. the saying on the size of the harvest in Jn 4:36). Both Jn 4:36 and 12:24 identify the harvest with the coming of non-Jewish converts.

There are several versions of the saying about loving and hating one's life (v. 25, Mk 8:35//Lk 9:24, Mt 10:39 and, in part, 16:25 and Lk 17:33). They all begin with the statement that a person who wishes to save his or her life will lose it, and then move to some version of the preservation of life by the one who loses it. The saying encapsulates the teaching about the suffering righteous, who is immortal, against the wicked, who will perish (cf. Wis 2-5). While some commentators have supposed that the contrast between "in this world" and eternal life was an addition, based on the dualism of the Evangelist, the same contrast belongs to the wisdom context (cf. Wis 5:13-15). This whole tradition played an important role in Christian understanding of the passion. John is probably using it when he insists that Jesus' testimony against the world leads to its rejection of him (cf. Wis 2:12-16. The wise man accuses the wicked of their sins; ·he is also said to have boasted that God is his father.). This saying may have been a traditional summary of the fate of the righteous person. When Jesus was seen to have been the suffering righteous, it could be associated with his death.

Prediction of the death of Jesus has always been linked with teaching on discipleship, as in the next saying (v. 26ab). Mark 8:34 has the discipleship saying before that, on losing/ saving one's life. John seems to have reformulated the traditional discipleship saying to reflect the language of the last discourses. The disciple who has shared Jesus' mission to the world will be honored (loved, share Jesus' glory) by the Father, as Jesus has been. These promises encapsulate the community's hope as it is spelled out in chapters 14–17.

John 12:27–36 *The Glorification of the Son of Man*

The final announcement of Jesus' passion includes divine testimony to the mission Jesus has completed. Jesus' turmoil at the arrival of the hour (v. 27) recalls the synoptic scenes of the agony in the garden (cp. Heb 5:9). John has no agony scene there. In the synoptics, Jesus prayed to be spared, but only if it was the Father's will. Here, that possibility is a hypothesis rejected by Jesus. In John, there is never any difference between the Father's will and that of Jesus. Instead, Jesus' prayer is for the hour which brings his glorification.

The Glory of the Messiah

A first-century Jewish work contains the following description of how the glory of the Lord will come upon a priestly messiah in the last days. Many of the themes in the rest of this chapter have parallels in that account, as the italics in the quotation show:

And he *shall execute a righteous judgment* upon the earth
    for many days
And his star shall arise in the heaven as of a king . . .
And he *shall shine forth as the sun* on the earth
And shall *remove all darkness* from under heaven,
And there shall be *peace* in all the earth.
And the *angels of the glory of the presence of the Lord*
    shall be glad in him [cp. Jn 1:51]
And the heavens shall be opened
And from the temple of *glory shall come upon him sanctification,*
With the Father's voice as from Abraham to Isaac,
And the *spirit of understanding and sanctification* shall
    rest upon him.
And *he will give the majesty of the Lord to his sons* in
    truth forevermore.
And *none shall succeed him for all generations forever.*
And in his priesthood *shall the Gentiles be multiplied*
    in knowledge upon the earth
In his priesthood shall *sin come to an end.*
And *Beliar* [= *Satan*] *shall be bound by him,*
And he shall give power to his children to tread evil spirits.
And *the Lord shall rejoice in his children;*
And all the *saints shall clothe themselves with joy.*

                                    [T Levi 18.2–14]

This passage is loaded with images that are found in the Fourth Gospel: judgment; sheds light upon the earth; angels rejoice in him (1:51); glory; sanctification; Father's voice gives glory to his sons (see 17:22); no successor; Satan is bound; sin ends; the Gentiles come to know God; the Lord rejoices in his children (chs. 14 and 17); the righteous have joy and peace (ch. 16). In the same document, the patriarch presents his sons with the following choice: "And now, my children, you have heard everything; choose therefore, for yourselves, either the light or the darkness; either the law of the Lord or the works of Beliar" (19.1). Jesus concludes this section and the chapter with a similar challenge. The large number of parallels suggests that John composed the chapter with such messianic imagery in mind.

We can also see that he must reinterpret it somewhat to fit the case of Jesus. The Father's voice comes to Jesus from heaven (v. 28), but it makes a somewhat unexpected announcement: "I have glorified it [= his name] and will glorify it again." The prayer that God will glorify his name (= "hallow his name" in the Lord's Prayer) was a request for the coming of the new age in which God's rule would be manifested to all people. Jesus' prayer and the second half of the divine statement imply that this is about to happen. "Have glorified it" presumably refers to the ministry of Jesus (cf. 17:4), which the Evangelist sees as the manifestation of the glory of God.

The crowd's understanding of the divine voice—either thunder or angels (v. 29)—may be "correct" in the Johannine sense if the Evangelist is invoking the imagery of the divine theophany at the end of the world: thunder; the Son of Man coming with the angels. Jesus' response announces that judgment. Both features of his pronouncement are paralleled in the passage quoted above: Satan is destroyed (v. 31) and the Gentiles are converted (v. 32). Although

John has cast this passion prediction in the first person, the crowd responds as though they had heard a third-person prediction of the suffering of the Son of Man, similar to the other passion predictions in John.

They protest Jesus' reference to "being lifted up" in light of the conviction—paralleled in the above quote—that the Messiah will remain forever. Jesus does not answer the question about the Son of Man directly, but if the imagery of the Messiah as light from the example is being alluded to, then Jesus clearly claims to be that light and to be departing. The crowd is encouraged to believe before it is too late (cp. Levi's exhortation to his sons). For the believer, the question of Jesus' eternal presence will be answered in the farewell discourses. Jesus remains forever, but not as people expect. Symbolically, Jesus concludes his appeal by doing what he has said he is about to; he withdraws (v. 36).

John 12:37-43 *Rejection of Jesus*

Despite his words and deeds, many did not believe in Jesus. John has prepared us for this outcome since the opening chapter (1:11). We may be so used to an atmosphere of skepticism and disagreement over what is said by a public figure that we do not face the difficulties posed by the rejection of Jesus. But look again at the description of the Messiah quoted in the last section. People are portrayed as streaming toward him in great numbers; those who do not believe are condemned in equally decisive fashion. The Evangelist has just invoked that image to present the earthly Jesus as the promised Messiah. He did not postpone being the Messiah until the end of the world, when he would do all the things the Jews expected. Rather, we are to see in him the true expression of everything the Messiah is—even if that means a radical change in the understanding of the

Messiah's role.

So the question must be answered: How can God's plan for the Messiah include rejection? First, the Evangelist does not hold the type of doctrine of predestination which would insist that some are *fated* not to believe. He has already given several types of explanation. Some are held from the light by their moral character (3:19-21, 5:40ff.). Even those who believe cannot take credit for their belief; they do so because God has drawn them (6:44-45, 10:29). But John clearly holds people responsible for their belief or lack of it. He speaks of the Father as drawing believers to Jesus because he is aware of the difficulties inherent in recognizing that Jesus is Messiah and Savior of the world.

John builds his case around two quotations from Isaiah, both of which remind his readers that God permits his prophets to be rejected; by implication, the case is not to be any different with the Messiah. The first (Is 53:1) comes right before a description of the suffering servant of God. At the same time, it reminds the Johannine reader that, no matter how incredible he finds it, Jesus teaches the revelation of the Father. Some find that revelation hard to accept because it is so different from what they had expected.

The second quotation (Is 6:10) was used in early Christianity to explain nonbelief (Acts 18:26f. Rm 11:8, Mt 13:13-15). God had warned the prophet at the beginning of his mission that people would not listen to his message. Christians understood the passage as a prophecy of Jesus' rejection. A true prophet, Isaiah had seen God's glory (Is 6). The Evangelist interprets that vision as a vision of the glory of Jesus and tells his readers that Isaiah spoke about Jesus (v. 41). People do not believe because they do not seek God's glory (vv. 42-45). The penalties against Christians—being put out of the synagogue—are too much for those who have status in the community, such as the Pharisees, to accept. Thus the believer is not to be unsettled by their lack of belief. God had predicted that would happen.

John 12:44–50 *The Judgment*

Many exegetes feel that these verses are a variant of 3:16–19 and a later addition to the gospel. However, the metaphor John has been using throughout requires some explanation of how Jesus has executed judgment. The description of the Messiah opened with the promise that he would execute judgment upon the earth for many days. Jesus is now presented as the one who has fulfilled that expectation. The themes are not new to the gospel. Belief in Jesus and belief in the Father are identified. Jesus is the light of the world (v. 46). Judgment is then explained as a function of the individual's response to the teaching of Jesus. Present and future elements of judgment expectation are combined. A person either accepts or rejects Jesus' teaching in the present and thus has his or her judgment, even though there will be a *day* of judgment as well (v. 48). John denies that the primary point of Jesus' mission is to judge (v. 47), but admits that those who expect judgment to result from the Messiah's activity are not entirely wrong. Jesus is the definitive and final revelation of the Father. A person must choose that revelation in order to be saved. The binary symbols, such as light and darkness, enable the Evangelist to establish that alternative clearly because such symbols do not admit a middle ground. It is either light or dark; a person is either alive or dead. The public ministry closes, then, with a strong assertion that Jesus' message is the message of the Father (v. 50). That statement may be seen as the correlate on the practical level of the identity between the Word and God, asserted in the prologue.

Much of the public ministry has been devoted to presenting Jesus as Savior of the world and Son of God. The Evangelist has had to make the case that all people are called to believe in Jesus and that Jesus is the final, complete revelation of the Father. The discourses which follow turn to another equally pressing question: Since Jesus has returned to the Father, what remains for the believers? They have not been rescued from evil by the end of the world. One approach in early Christianity was to assume that Jesus would soon return to carry out the expected messianic tasks; the believer only had to endure until that end (cf. Mk 13). John presents a different view. Jesus does not leave his disciples with an apocalyptic promise but with a way to exist in the world, however long it may continue.

PART THREE
Farewell Discourses

13. The Last Supper

The Johannine account of the Last Supper contains no account of the institution of the Eucharist. Instead, Jesus performs the symbolic act of washing the disciples' feet. A variety of theories has been proposed to explain the lack of a eucharistic scene. Some suppose that John's tradition did not know the story of the institution of the Eucharist at the supper but supposed it to have taken place during the public ministry. Others claim that John was against sacraments; still others that the Eucharist had become a mystery which could not be described in public. The most reasonable suggestion seems to be that John understood the Eucharist as a key sign of Jesus' Messiahship and used the traditional, early Christian association of the bread with manna to link his eucharistic teaching and the loaves miracle in chapter 6. Similarly, he has presented baptism and its gift of the Spirit as the true meaning of messianic expectations about the gift of running water.

We presume that the Evangelist also knew an independent tradition that Jesus had washed the disciples' feet as an example of humility, which they are to follow (vv. 4–5, 12–13a, 14–15, 17). The Evangelist has framed that scene with traditions about the betrayal (vv. 2, 10b–11, 18–19, 21ff.) and expanded it with dialogue and traditional material about discipleship in order to tie the foot washing to the death of Jesus. This combination of different traditional materials has led commentators to a variety of hypotheses about the composition of the scene; Brown, for example, sees evidence of two editions by the Evangelist (2:599–62), while Schnackenburg (3:7–15) has suggested extensive reworking by the redactor. We favor the view that the Evangelist has combined a variety of traditions: foot-washing scene, stories about Judas, and discipleship sayings.

The Johannine account also raises a chronological problem: the meal is not a Passover meal. Indeed, Jesus was executed and buried before the Passover. References throughout the Johannine passion narrative show that his tradition has all the events of the passion occur before the Passover (cf. 18:28, 19:14). The Evangelist *does* share the early Christian theological tradition which compared Jesus and the paschal lamb. He is condemned while the paschal lambs are slaughtered in the temple; like the lambs, none of his bones are broken (19:36). Thus John has drawn a direct analogy between the fate of the two victims, rather than between the two meals.

John 13:1-5 *The Foot Washing*

Verse 1 introduces the entire last section of the gospel; it will be dominated by the motif of Jesus' love for his disciples—the mode in which Jesus remains present with them. The meaning of "his own" is different here than in 1:11, where "his own" reject the Word. Here it recalls the relationship between the shepherd and his sheep (10:3f., 12-14, 27).

Jesus' prediction of his betrayal at the supper comes from his pre-Johannine tradition (cp. Lk 22:3). John 13:27 was probably the traditional location of that prediction, but the Evangelist expanded the betrayal motif so that the reader is reminded throughout of the story of Satan's activity against Jesus. The "hour" is Jesus' victory over Satan (12:31).

Verse 3 resumes the narrative. The Evangelist picks up the metaphor of Jesus as God's agent; "who had handed everything over to him" refers to the commissioning of the agent with the authority of the one who sends him (cf. 3:35).

John frequently uses this metaphor in connection with the believers as the ones who are given over to Jesus. None of them is to be lost (6:39, 10:29). The conclusion of this verse introduces a new motif: now it is time for the agent to return to the one who sent him. We already know, from verse 1, what the report on his mission will be: "He loved his own in the world, and would show his love for them to the end."

The foot washing would have been somewhat shocking. Disciples of the rabbis are said to have washed their master's feet as a sign of devotion; but it was an action one could not demand of one's slave if he were Jewish (midr. Mekilta Exod xxi 2). Thus Jesus' action is contrary to custom (cp. Lk 12:37, where Jesus speaks of a master waiting on his servants). John gives this scene a more complex significance, rather than merely making it an example of humility. After the resurrection, it was understood as a symbol of Jesus' death. It also defines the new community that is brought into being by Jesus, in that it stipulates the type of relationships that are to exist between members of that group. Further, it serves as part of the commissioning of the disciples. At the same time, we are constantly reminded of Judas, who will not have any share in that community.

John 13:6-11 *Dialogue with Peter*

John follows his usual pattern of beginning the interpretation of Jesus' action with a dialogue based on misunderstandings. Peter protests that Jesus, the master, should not perform such a task (v. 6). Indeed, he could hardly be considered a good disciple had he felt otherwise. When Peter is told that he will understand later—after the resurrection (v. 7; cp. 2:27, 12:16)—he still does not understand. He thinks that "afterward" means as soon as Jesus has completed action (v. 8a). But when Jesus tells Peter that, unless he submits, he cannot continue to be with Jesus after Jesus' return to the Father (cp. 14:3, 17:24), Peter responds enthusiastically by volunteering for a whole bath (v. 9). Although he still does not understand what Jesus is saying, Peter's response is quite different from that of the nonbelievers in John. He does not go away discouraged but responds enthusiastically, with the best of his understanding.

Verse 10 is one of the most difficult in the gospel. The form of the saying in 10a occurs frequently in John (3:29, 4:35a, 37, 8:35). In each case, John was either quoting a well-known proverb or creating one on the basis of custom. Verse 10a is such a proverbial saying, which rejects Peter's proposal. Like the earlier sayings of this type, it points out that Jesus is referring to the time of salvation brought by his coming, and not to the act of foot washing. The rest of the verse rather awkwardly elaborates the saying to reintroduce the theme of the disciple who betrays Jesus. The Evangelist must guard against the possible misunderstanding that would include Judas among those who were cleansed and promised a future with Jesus.

John 13:12-20 *Commissioning the Disciples*

The second interpretation indicates that having a share with Jesus does not simply direct the disciples toward some future salvation; it also dictates how they must relate to one another and it points out that they, in turn, will be sent, just as Jesus had been.

Discipleship as Service

The service commanded among the disciples has parallels

in the synoptic tradition. Jesus counters disputes among the
disciples with a saying about service (Mk 10:45, Mt 20:28.
Note that the Son of Man serves by dying, a theme picked
up by John. Luke 22:26f. locates the teaching about discipleship and service in the context of the Last Supper).
John reflects a common Christian tradition, which understood Jesus' death to have specific implications for the
relationships between Christians. They cannot act on human
standards of honor and greatness, since Jesus has rejected
those. Rather, Christians must relate to one another on the
basis of an equality that is not based on a philosophical
principle about equality between people but on the desire
to relate to others in service. As in the case here, that service
may even require laying aside some justified claims to honor
and respect. The Evangelist is careful to guard against interpreting Jesus' action—or his death—in a way that would
suggest that he did not deserve the honor paid him.

The Disciples Are Sent as Jesus Was

Framed by two synoptic-like sayings, verses 16-20 draw
a further implication from Jesus' action: The disciples must
not only deal with each other as Jesus has dealt with them,
they must also be sent. This motif will be picked up in the
discourses which follow. As he is about to return to the
Father, Jesus must designate those who are to represent him
to the world, his disciples. The traditional saying in verse
16 is similar to Mt 10:24//Lk 6:40. Perhaps he knew a two-
part saying similar to Mk 10:24, since the earlier context
has the teacher/disciple contrast. John 15:20 quotes the
first part of this saying. But the Evangelist has reformulated
the saying to introduce the messenger language about the
one who is sent. Although an agent may be considered
identical with the one who sent him, he is never considered

greater. The macarism in verse 17 underlines the exemplary application of the foot washing: The disciple must act like Jesus, who sends him.

But, again, the Evangelist must make a qualification. Jesus' commissioning does not extend to ´all the disciples; one will betray him. The citation from Ps 41:9 was part of the tradition about the betrayal (cf. Mk 14:18). As John uses it, however, the wording is slightly different. Jesus refers to the one who breaks "my bread." This adaptation heightens the allusion to a solemn table fellowship, which the betrayer is violating. It also stresses Jesus' initiative in providing the bread—just as he did in the eucharistic scene (6:11). Verse 18 explains the prediction. The betrayal is not to shake the disciples' faith in Jesus' divinity. The divine I AM in Jn 8:28 asserted that the crucifixion would reveal the truth of Jesus' claim. But in a presentation which has stressed the divinity of Jesus, his closeness to the Father, and his control over what happens to him, betrayal by a disciple must have raised some problems. John spends more time on that motif than does any other gospel. It was introduced at the conclusion of chapter 6 (v. 70), the chapter on the Eucharist, and is a consistent motif in this chapter on the Last Supper. Several explanations are offered: Judas is possessed by Satan; his moral character is questionable. At the same time, Jesus is aware that these negative factors are part of the larger picture that will lead to his glorification. He, at least, is not surprised by what happens; so the disciples should not be either.

Another traditional saying concludes the foot-washing scene (v. 20; cp. Mk 10:40). Some commentators suppose this verse to be out of place, but John is using it to continue the commissioning of the disciples. The agent is to be received like the one who sent him: Jesus like the Father; the disciples like Jesus.

John 13:21-30 *Judas Departs*

Judas finally leaves the circle of the disciples. The remark that Jesus is troubled at what is coming recalls 12:27. It may have been part of John's tradition as an allusion to Ps 42:5 (cf. Mk 14:34). The prediction of the betrayal is almost identical with Mk 14:18//Mt 26:21, except that it has the Johannine double Amen and omits the Scripture quote which follows in the other versions (John used that quotation in v. 18). The descriptions of the disciples' reactions vary. In Mk 14:19, each wonders if he is referred to; they question Jesus directly. In Lk 22:23, they question each other. Here (vv. 22, 24) they question each other and Jesus. His answer in Mark states only that one of those at the meal is the betrayer. In John (cp. Mt), Jesus explicitly identifies Judas. He had previously associated Judas with Satan (6:71). The explanation that Judas acted under Satan's influence was apparently traditional (cp. Lk 22:3), as was the reference to darkness (Lk 22:53). The Evangelist has set these traditions in a compact scene which makes two points. First, Jesus' real adversary in his "hour" is Satan (12:31, 14:30). Second, although Satan might seem to be winning by getting one of Jesus' disciples to betray him, Jesus is in control of what happens (v. 26).

Further, John counterbalances this negative image of failed discipleship with a new character, the beloved disciple. He is as close to Jesus as Jesus was said to have been to the Father (v. 23; cp. 1:18). This is the first mention of that disciple. Some interpreters suppose that John means him to be a symbol of the ideal disciple. However, Jn 19:35 and 21:24 show that the Johannine Church looked back to him as the source of its tradition. The "Beloved disciple" is always associated with Peter. While some have supposed that John is hostile to the Petrine tradition, Schnackenburg's suggestion (3:38) that John wishes to associate his Church's tradition with the developing authority of the Petrine tradition seems more reasonable. The two are always portrayed as friends and associates. John brings this scene to a close by announcing that night has arrived. We have been expecting the coming darkness to signal the end of Jesus' ministry (9:4, 11:10).

John 13:31-38 *Jesus' True Disciples*

Now that Judas has departed, Jesus begins to instruct his true disciples. These verses introduce a discourse which continues to the end of chapter 14.

The Testament

In composing these chapters, the Evangelist uses a literary genre that was widespread in Jewish literature of his day: the testament, or instructions of the dying patriarch to his sons. The disciples are addressed as "little children" in verse 33. (This is the only use of the term in the gospel, though its frequency in 1 John suggests that it was used within the Johannine community.) This expression fits the testament genre of the dying patriarch who addresses his children.

The OT provided models for such testaments (e.g., Gn 47:29-49, Jacob; Dt 32-34, Moses; cp. Jos., *Ant* IV viii, 45-47). Testaments composed around the time of Jesus for each of the twelve patriarchs are preserved in a work known as the *Testaments of the Twelve Patriarchs* and in fragments of individual testaments from Qumran. Parts of larger works also contained testaments. Elsewhere in the NT we find testaments of Paul (Acts 20:17-38, 2 Tm 3:1-4:8) and Peter

(2 Pt). Such works usually open with an announcement of the imminent death of the speaker. His instructions to his sons may include reflection on his life as an example for them, as well as admonishments to keep the law in the future. Often the patriarch predicts the trials to come upon his descendants, and may conclude with a prayer or blessing upon them. The reader of Jn 14–17 can easily find parallels to all these features of a testament or farewell discourse. Brown (2: 597–601) suggests comparison with even more minute details of such works. We have already seen that, earlier in the chapter, the disciples were commissioned to carry on Jesus' mission. John's adoption of the testament genre for Jesus' last words with the disciples and the designation "little children" place them in the position of being Jesus' heirs as well.

The Son of Man Is Glorified

The fivefold announcement that the time for Jesus' glorification had come (v. 3f.) indicated the arrival of the "hour," which had been publicly announced earlier (12:23, 27f., 31). These announcements show a peculiar mix of past and future tenses (cp. 12:28). Such mixed tenses, which occur throughout the discourses, make it seem as though Jesus speaks from the perspective of one who has already passed into glory. Although the crucifixion/exaltation still lies ahead of him, Jesus speaks as the glorified one. This literary technique is yet another way in which the Evangelist can bring home his point that Jesus' "hour" is his exaltation. Exaltation is not simply a reward Jesus gets for obedience to God's will to the point of death. If it were, Jesus would not be any different from other righteous people to whom the words of Wis 5 might be applied. But John has already made it clear that Jesus' death is not like that of any other righteous person or martyr; it is linked to the gift of the Spirit, to eternal life, to the salvation of the Gentiles, and to the revelation of Jesus' divine identity.

Though the announcement of impending death might be expected in a testament, the vocabulary is typically Johannine: "little while," departure, seeking Jesus. A similar saying about Jesus' departure and attempts to seek him was used as a judgment oracle against the Jews (7:33f., 8:21). Misunderstanding of the earlier sayings had led to ironically correct conclusions about the mission to the Greeks and Jesus' control over his death. Now the disciples are the ones who misunderstand. Their misunderstanding leads to explanations of where Jesus is going and how they—unlike the nonbelievers—will be able to follow.

Love Command

The exchange between Jesus and the disciples is interrupted by two verses about the new commandment of love (34f; cf. 15:12, 17, 1 John shows that this command was the key to the community's understanding of relationships between members; cf. 1 Jn 2:7, 3:11, 23.). Some interpreters (e.g., Schnackenburg, 3:59) argue that these verses were a later addition to the gospel.

This passage defines the Christian community as the one in which the love between its members can even be recognized by outsiders "all," v. 35). John is speaking about love as a characteristic of relationships between Christians and not as a universal imperative. The Essene rule also commanded fraternal love (I QS i. 9–11). The love command is new, not because it cannot be found in the OT (cf. Lv 19:18) but because the community in which it is operative is the community of the new covenant (cp. I QS i. 8; iii. 11f.). But John's understanding of the love command goes beyond the Qumran-type use of the command as a characteristic of the new community because the command is grounded in the action and example of Jesus (v. 34; cp. 15:12) and even of God himself (3:16; cp. 1 Jn 4:7–9). The foundation of that command gives it an ethical seriousness and significance within the Johannine community that it did not have at Qumran, where it is merely one command among many. More than anything, it is the mark of the Christian community.

John has turned the prediction of Peter's denial (Mk 14:29 parr.) into a dialogue based on his misunderstanding of Jesus' statement that the disciples cannot follow him (vv. 36–38). The gospels agree in having Peter express a willingness to die rather than deny Jesus; in John, he says he will "give his life" for Jesus. Since the reader knows that Jesus is about to give his life *for* his sheep (10:11) and the people (11:51ff.), Peter's offer to give his life *for* Jesus seems almost ludicrous. Nevertheless, the Evangelist and his readers knew that Peter eventually followed Jesus through martyrdom (v. 36b, 21:18).

14. Jesus, the Way to the Father

This chapter consoles the disciples with explanations of how Jesus will continue to be present after his return to the Father. Throughout the gospel the Evangelist has given new interpretations of traditional Christian language about judgment which locate judgment in the present life of the believer. The farewell discourses take a similar approach.

In the synoptic gospels, Jesus' last teaching focused on the coming judgment and his return as Son of Man. The persecutions that were predicted for the disciples were seen as part of the larger scheme of woes that had to come before the end of the age. Such apocalyptic predictions consoled and encouraged Christians. The believer could see that everything that happened to him or her was part of a plan which will lead inevitably to the glorious return of Jesus, a return that would vindicate their belief before the whole world.

The Fourth Evangelist has a different approach to such questions. The return of Jesus, which is to vindicate Christian faith, has already occurred in the experience of the Christian community. One does not have to wait either for heaven or for the second coming to see the fulfillment of Jesus' promises. John's reinterpretation of Christian eschatological language also reminds us that Christianity is not a technique for "getting into heaven." Although the believer may certainly expect a future life, his or her attention is focused on the present.

John 14:1-5 *The Return*

Just as Jesus had been troubled at the beginning of his

157

"hour" (12:27), his departure will trouble the disciples. This section of the discourse, which began at 13:31, opens with a call to the faith, which must overcome the doubts of the disciples. Belief in Jesus and the Father is the condition for the "return" which Jesus is promising (vv. 7, 9). As in many of the earlier discourses, John begins with a statement of the tradition, the "earthly" or "lesser" things, which everyone should be able to grasp, before he moves on to his reinterpretation. Verses 2–3 state the traditional eschatological view that Jesus will return at the parousia and take his followers to dwelling places reserved for the righteous in heaven. Jews of the time could speak of heaven as God's house (Philo, *de somn,* i. 43; *confus ling,* 78). Apocalyptic visions of heaven described the dwelling places of the righteous and the wicked (I En 39.4f., 41.2, IV Ez 7.80, 101). John 21:22 shows that the expression "to come" refers to the parousia. Schnackenburg (3:70) points out that verse 3 may be a translation into Johannine language of our earliest example of parousia expectations, in 1 Thes 4:16f.:

a) "He will descend from heaven" becomes "I will come again."

b) "We will be snatched up to meet him in the air" becomes "I will take you to myself."

c) "We will always be with the Lord" becomes "where I am you also will be."

Thus we may suppose that Jn 14:3 is a traditional formulation of Christian expectation about the last judgment as it was known in John's community.

In order to move from the tradition to his interpretation, the Evangelist provides a misunderstanding. (Had Jesus been addressing Jewish opponents, the central role he played in these expectations would have been the point of difficulty, but now he is addressing those who have accepted him as the Messiah.) The transition is provided by Jesus' assertion

that the disciples know the "way" to the place he is going
(v. 4). Thomas misunderstands. He claims that he does not
know where Jesus is going—despite the fact that the language
of verses 2f. is common in Jewish sources—let alone know
how to get there (v. 5). Again, it is typical of Johannine
style that the question put to Jesus is more obtuse than the
situation warrants. The interpretation takes for granted that
heaven is the goal. It focuses, instead, on the "way."

John 14:6-11 *Jesus as the Way*

Jesus answers with a solemn I AM pronouncement. He is
the way about which Thomas asks (v. 6a). An epexegetical
"and" joins two nouns to "the way," which tell us that it
is "truth" and "life"; for example, the truth revealed by
Jesus leads to life (5:26, 10:10, 28, 11:25f.). Both the Essenes (I QS xix. 17f., 21; CD i. 3) and the early Christians
(Acts 9:2, 19:9, 22:4) referred to their respective communities
as the way. John may be applying that community designation to Jesus. Verse 6b makes the Evangelist's position even
clearer: Jesus is not just one possible route to salvation,
he is the only one possible. Throughout the gospel, Jesus
has claimed to be the only mode of revelation and the fulfillment of all hopes of salvation.

Verses 7-11 explain the mode of coming to the Father,
made possible by Jesus. To know Jesus is to know the
Father (v. 9; cp. 12:45). Verse 10b uses the image of Jesus
as like the Father who sent him. Although the first part of
verse 7 could be read simply as a promise of a future vision
of the Father, 7b makes it clear that the Evangelist has
something more in mind. The expression *ap'arti* has been
the subject of some controversy. Does it mean "from now
on" (e.g., Brown, 2:631)? If so, it is from the time of the

glorification that the disciples will know the Father. The difficulty with that interpretation lies in the expression "you have seen him," which occurs in the second half of the clause. Schnackenburg (3:76) points to the use of the same expression at 13:19 to mean "already." Therefore, the Evangelist is saying that the disciples know and have seen the Father through Jesus.

That interpretation provides a natural lead into the explanation that is given after Philip asks to be shown the Father: Whoever has seen/heard Jesus has seen/heard the Father. Verse 10a presents the mutual relationship of Jesus in the Father and the Father in Jesus as something the disciples believe. That relationship is explained by pointing out that Jesus is the agent of the Father (v. 10b; cp. 8:26, 12:49). The end of verse 10 is rather unusual; it suggests that there is more to the relationship between Jesus and the Father than might be expected on the basis of the agent metaphor. We had been told that Jesus does the works of the Father (10:39); here it is said that the Father, remaining in Jesus, does his works. Many commentators assume that this formulation is equivalent to verse 10b or to earlier statements about Jesus' works. However, John uses "to remain" of very specific demands for belief. In 5:38, the Word of God is said not to remain in the Jews because they do not believe that Jesus is from the Father. John 6:56 promises that the person who partakes of the Eucharist will remain in Jesus and Jesus will remain in him.

This type of expression recurs in the vine metaphor of chapter 15, where a mutual indwelling is promised the disciple (15:5; cp. 1 Jn 3:24).

Finally 8:31 promised some Jews who believed in Jesus that if they remained in him they would truly be his disciples and know the truth that would make them free. John 1:39 and 4:40 use expressions about remaining with Jesus as part of the language of conversion—the new disciple "remains" with Jesus. Thus John seems to use "remain in" in controversy situations to characterize true faith in Jesus as something which cannot be shaken: The disciple cannot be separated from Jesus.

We suggest that the expression serves a similar function here. It is always possible to suspect an agent of "free lancing"—of doing some things on his own that are not part of the assignment. The expression in 10c excludes such a possibility by suggesting a permanent presence of the Father in/with Jesus. Although Jesus has been "sent" by the Father, he has not been separated from the Father, as an earthly envoy would have been. Verse 11 then rounds off this section with another command to believe (cp. 13:1). The command at least to believe in the works, if not the indwelling, of Father and Son has a parallel at 10:38, where it follows a discussion about the unity between Jesus and the Father. Even if a person finds John's description of the relationship between Jesus and God difficult, he or she should be able to believe that he was sent on the basis of the ministry.

John 14:12–14 *Prayer in the Name of Jesus*

The discourse turns toward the life of the disciples after Jesus' departure and takes up traditional motifs about prayer. The synoptics have other groups of sayings about the power of prayer (Mk 11:22b–27//Mt 21:21f, Mt 17:17f.). Many commentators point to the synoptic promises that the disciples will work miracles (Lk 17:6//Mt 17:20) as parallels to the "greater works" in verse 12. However, we have seen that John always explains his "greater" in the following verses. The disciples have been told, in effect, that they are to carry on Jesus' works when he returns to the Father; i.e., they are being commissioned to act as his agents in the world (cp. 13:20). Just as Jesus' ministry had glorified the Father (12:28), the disciples' mission (teaching about Jesus?) will glorify the Father through the Son (v. 13b).

We have already seen that the Johannine view of the Son as agent implies a unique identity between the two. Subsequent verses in this discourse will detail the relationship between Father, Son, and disciples, which is necessary to make the agency of the disciples possible. We have also seen that prayer, in the context of Jesus' relationship to the Father, becomes a statement of Jesus' identity with the Father (11:41b-42, 12:27f., ch. 17). Here, too, the prayer of the disciple may be said to express the Father/Son identity. John explains that the faith required is in Jesus; it is not just confidence that "prayer works." He recasts the part on giving so that Jesus is the one who acts on behalf of the disciples (vv. 13a, 14). Thus the Father is still being glorified by the activity of the Son when the disciples carry on their mission in Jesus' name (v. 13b). The sayings about prayer in 15:7, 16, 16:23f. are more traditional. The Father answers prayer in Jesus' name. The sayings probably represent the type of tradition the Evangelist has reformulated in this passage.

John 14:15-24 *Love of Jesus and His Return*

Having told his disciples that his departure is beneficial to them, Jesus picks up on the theme of love, introduced at 13:34ff. This characteristic of the community explains how Jesus remains present with the disciples after his departure. The command to love Jesus, which is found here, is unusual. Generally, one is exhorted to love God or others (13:34) and to believe in Jesus (14:11). This section divides into sub-sections on the basis of the repeated saying about love of Jesus and keeping his commandments (vv. 15, 21, 23). The Evangelist seems to have woven together a variety of in-dependent sayings about the return of Jesus. He does not provide a systematic account of all the possible varieties of indwelling or return suggested by these sayings. Through-out, we find expressions reminiscent of traditional eschatology to express a mode of presence which clearly does not require the end of the world.

Jesus first promises to ask the Father to send the Para-clete/Spirit of Truth to the disciples (vv. 16f.). The Jo-hannine writings show varied uses of the Paraclete tradition (cf. the section on Paraclete). The different Paraclete sayings cannot be harmonized into a single picture, as many com-mentators have tried to do (cf. see the remarks of Schnack-enburg, 3:84f.). The Evangelist seems to have composed this passage for readers already familiar with the Paraclete figure, since—unlike the other passages—no particular func-tions are ascribed to him. Both sayings in this chapter (vv. 16f., 26) have assimilated the Paraclete image to that of the Holy Spirit. In both, the Father sends the Paraclete at Jesus' request. The expression "another Paraclete" in verse 16 has been a continual puzzle. Some commentators have tried to link it to Jesus as heavenly Paraclete in 1 Jn 2:1ff., but its use in connection with the departure of Jesus clearly links it to the earthly Jesus. In some sense, the Paraclete must be understood as taking over for Jesus with respect to the Christian community. The manuscript evidence is divided as to whether 17c should read "will be" or "is" in you. Recent editors have selected the latter as more likely. It may be a parenthetical remark by the Evangelist, intended to remind his readers that this promise is present in the community; it is not a past event.

The promise not to leave the disciples "orphans" reminds us of the testament genre in which the patriarch addresses his children (cp. 13:33). The mode of return that is introduced in this saying shows a similar structure to what has been said about the Paraclete: Jesus will return to his disciples, but not in such a way that the world will witness his return (v. 19). His return will establish a new mode of presence with the disciples (v. 20). Because that presence seems to be understood as continuing, it is difficult to see the return as merely a reference to the resurrection appearances, even though Mt 28:20 ends such an appearance with a promise of eternal presence. This passage in John may represent further reflection on such traditions about the eternal presence of Jesus. Verse 19 promises the disciples life on the basis of Jesus' life—a motif that had been symbolically elaborated in the Lazarus story of chapter 11 (cp. 5:24, 6:57, 17:2).

The first subsection concludes with a solemn pronouncement (v. 20). Its form echoes both a prophetic eschatological saying and the famous Johannine I-Am sayings. We are reminded of 8:28—when Jesus is lifted up, his divine I AM will become known—and 10:38: belief in Jesus' works will teach a person that Jesus is in the Father. The expression "on that day" commonly refers to the parousia. Some suggest that "seeing Jesus again" also comes from a parousia tradition, like Rv 1:7: "Behold he comes with clouds and every eye shall see him." But John is not promising such a universal appearance of Jesus. In fact, every eye will not see him; only the believers' will.

It is frequently suggested that John is using "on that day" to refer to Easter. We propose that he has merely taken it over from the tradition as an appropriate introduction to a solemn pronouncement. The knowledge called for here is most like that in 10:38b, where the expression "the

Father is in me and I am in the Father" concludes a public-controversy discourse in which Jesus has been defending his divinity. This saying alludes to the previous formulation of the relationship between Jesus and the disciples—on that between himself and the Father. The agency metaphor has been expanded to include the disciples. Those who keep Jesus' commandments (vv. 15, 21) may be characterized as having the same close relationship with Jesus as Jesus has with the Father. We should not read these expressions of indwelling as references to some private, individualistic mystical awareness. Throughout the gospel, Jesus' agency has been shown in the works he does "from" the Father. The disciples too must respond to their status with appropriate conduct. Johannine expressions about knowing God retain overtones of the OT traditions in which "knowledge of God" means keeping his commandments. Here, knowing God implies fulfillment of Jesus' commandments.

Verse 21 continues the motif of loving Jesus and keeping his commandments. One does not love God by having sentimental feelings about him, but by doing what is commanded. Jesus and the Father will love the person who keeps Jesus' commandments, and Jesus will manifest himself to him and her. Thus this verse condenses what has been said in verses 15–20. Perhaps the Evangelist created it as a transition into the following question about the "seeing" language that Jesus has been using.

Jesus is asked to explain how he can appear to the disciples and not to the world. Schnackenburg (3:92) points out that there may be an apologetic motif behind these verses. Later opponents of Christianity objected that Jesus should have manifested himself to enemies and not just friends (con Cel II, 63–67; GPet 38–42). Perhaps John inserted this question to answer such an objection. The variation on the previous saying in verse 23 is the high point of the language about indwelling. The use of the word dwelling refers back to the traditional language about dwellings in heaven in verse 3. The verse reinterprets that language to suggest that what really counts is not being taken to some heavenly location in the future but the presence of Father and Son among the believers. The Evangelist may also be alluding to OT promises that God will dwell with his people in the last days (e.g., Zec 2:14, Ez 27:26f.). Verse 24 answers the question. Jesus does not return to the world, because it does not love him and does not keep his commandments (cf. 8:42). Once again we are reminded that Jesus was the one sent by God to deliver the Father's message, not his own.

John 14:25–31 *Jesus' Departure*

With the expression "these things I have spoken . . . " (a refrain that will recur in 15:11, 16:1, 4a 25, 33), Jesus moves to leave. The time for his earthly revelation is over (cp. 12:36b on the public ministry). But the disciples do not have to worry that they will not be able to carry on without Jesus. The Paraclete, here identified with the Holy Spirit, will teach the disciples "all things," which the Evangelist explains as reminding them of everything Jesus had said to them. We have seen that "remembering" in John (e.g., 12:16) is a technical term for the insight the disciples were able to gain after the resurrection. It is usually tied to the realization that Jesus has fulfilled the OT. The Evangelist is not suggesting that the Spirit makes the disciples omniscient or gives them new revelation; rather, the Spirit will guarantee them true understanding of Jesus' words and ministry. (Schnackenburg [3:96] points out that the Evangelist is not concerned with linking the gift of the Spirit to some church office—the Johannine community does not seem to have developed a structure of church offices as yet. Rather, he uses the disciples throughout as symbolic of later Christians.)

The concluding gift of peace suggests fulfillment of the eschatological promise of peace (Is 5:27, Ez 37:26). Elsewhere in the NT, peace is also linked to the coming of Jesus (Lk 2:14, 19:38, 42). In Jn 20:19, 21, peace is a gift that the risen Jesus gives the disciples. The antithesis between the disciples and the world, which has dominated this discourse, returns in the saying about peace. Jesus' peace cannot be compared with that bestowed by the world. The OT promises of eschatological peace cannot be understood as fulfilled by Jesus if they are taken as referring to the obliteration of conflict from the world or from the life of the believer. John warns us that we should not expect our religion to be some sort of supertherapy or problem-solving mechanism. The disciple must find a different sort of peace, which is not based on such concerns.

Jesus repeats his opening injunction that the disciples should rejoice over his return to the Father (v. 27c; cf. v. 1). The expression "for the Father is greater than I" continues to cause problems in the interpretation of Christology (see Schnackenburg, 3:98). Some use it as clear evidence for the view that Jesus was subordinate to the Father, but Brown (2:654f.) correctly points out that this expression derives from the agent metaphor which is used everywhere in the gospel. Compare the proverb quoted in 13:16: "No messenger is greater than the one who sent him." In Jn 14:28, the Father is greater in the sense that everything Jesus does is derived from the Father (4:12, 8:53, 5:20, 10:29). Jesus does not do anything on his own. If he did, Christianity would be open to the Jewish charge of blasphemy, or believing in two gods.

Verse 30a, "I will no longer speak many things to you" (NAB: "I shall not go on speaking to you longer"), suggests that this discourse was, at one stage, an independent composition. Perhaps there was an earlier edition of John in which chapters 15-17 did not follow chapter 14 (see Brown, 2:586-93; Schnackenburg, 3:99). Or the Evangelist may have worked out the four discourses, found in these chapters, as independent units prior to putting them in the gospel. In the latter case, it is nevertheless difficult to see what led him to retain the conclusion at verse 31. Why not have Jesus get up to go at the end of chapter 17? Therefore, some suggest that though the Evangelist composed all four discourses, he included only the first in his gospel. After his death, a disciple put the others here to prevent their being lost. (This is essentially Brown's view. Schnackenburg tries to argue that disciple(s) composed the later discourses, using chapter 14 as a model.)

Victory over Satan

Jesus' impending victory over Satan was announced at 13:31. Now Satan's approach—paralleling that of Judas?—signals the time for the crucifixion. But the Evangelist never lets us forget that Jesus' death is under his/God's control. It is not a victory for the forces of evil in the world. Jesus explains that his death will prove his love for God and his perfect fulfillment of his will (cp. 8:28, 10:18, 12:49). Brown 2:656) points out that this is the only place in the NT where Jesus is explicitly said to love the Father. (Of course, carrying out God's will, as Jesus does, is loving God in the biblical sense.) We suggest, further, that the expression derives from the meditation on the fate of the righteous person found in Wis 2-5, which formed an important part of John's understanding of Jesus (cf. 12:25). There, the death of the righteous man at the hands of evil people tests/

proves his love for God and his obedience to God's commandments, even though the evil think that they have proved the righteous person wrong about God.

This conclusion provides us with the perspective from which the entire discourse is composed. John had consistently contrasted betrayal with the love command and the new conditions of discipleship in his description of the earlier part of the meal (cf. the foot washing and its interpretation). Once the betrayer had left, Jesus turned to instruct the disciples. This discourse answers problems that this betrayal and Jesus' death will create. What happens to Jesus' ministry after he has died? Does his death prove that the Jews were right when they said that he was not from God but a false prophet and a blasphemer? Why didn't Jesus return with the angels as Son of Man and prove to the world that he and the Christians who were faithful to him were right?

Wisdom 5:1-16 ends with a dramatic recognition scene in which the wicked see the righteous enthroned as judge. Thus righteousness is vindicated. But Jesus does not show himself to his enemies at all. First, the disciples are assured that the death of Jesus is a return to God. Jesus dies as a .righteous person, not as a sinful one. Second, the return of Jesus is for the disciples—those who love him and keep his commandments. Third, that return means that the disciples, in their turn, are agents: Jesus dwells in them; they do "greater" works. Insofar as the world sees Jesus at all, it must do so in the community that bears witness to him. Note that John is not talking individualistic language; the community as a whole is witness (cf. 13:35).

Finally, one must not suppose that Satan rules this world until the end, making it difficult for the righteous person to persevere. Jesus has overcome the "ruler of this world." The unity between the disciples and Jesus, which is at the basis of their witness, also assures them a share in that victory. All four points apply as well today as they did in the first century; and we may ask ourselves how well the Christian community measures up to the implied responsibilities.

15. The True Vine

Chapter 16 will prove to be a different version of many themes that are associated with the departure of Jesus in the previous discourse, but this chapter is not tied to the departure theme. It focuses on the position of the community. Its treatment of the fate of Christians in the world (15:18–16: 4a) has parallels with the missionary instructions of Mt 10:17–25 (see the chart in Brown, 2:694). Although some have argued that the discourses in chapters 15–17 were the work of disciples of the Evangelist, we treat them as independent compositions by the Evangelist himself. This discourse shows typical features of Johannine composition when it is compared with chapter 10. Both apply an OT metaphor for Israel to Jesus. Both turn a single parable into a double one and follow that parable with several interpretations. Each chapter concludes with an indication of hostility and opposition. Both chapters, then, have been composed according to the same plan.

The Vine Image

The OT prophets used images of vines and vineyards to describe Israel. The nation is usually compared to a good vine or vineyard which has been carefully tended by God but has gone to ruin anyway and has failed to yield fruit (e.g., Is 5:1–7, 27:2–6, Jer 2:21, Ez 15:1–6, 19:10–14, Ps 80:8–15). Some NT parables (Mk 12:1–11 parr.) pick up this imagery. John typically takes images that apply to Israel and attaches them to Jesus. In this particular case, John may have read such an application from Ps 80, where God is asked to re-

store his vine, Israel, which had been devastated by her
enemies (vv. 14-16), and then to strengthen his chosen one,
the Son of Man (vv. 17-18). This juxtaposition led to a
change in the text—also followed in the Greek translations—
which introduced a phrase about the Son of Man from
5:18 into 5:16. The LXX of verses 15-16 reads:

> Look down from heaven and see,
> and consider this vine,
> and restore that which thy right hand planted;
> and [look down] upon [the] Son of Man,
> whom you strengthened for yourself.

Although the psalm clearly applies the vine image to the
people of Israel, the close association of vine and Son of
Man might have led the Evangelist to the formulation of
the I-Am saying, identifying the two.

Early Christianity associated the vine with the Eucharist
(e.g., Mk 14:25, Did 9:4). John 12:24 connects bearing
fruit with Jesus' death. John 15:13 links the vine image to
the death of Jesus (cp. 6:51), and language about "remaining" in Jesus is part of the eucharistic teaching in 6:56.
Brown (2:673) suggests that the same background in Jewish
wisdom literature lies behind 6:51-58 and the use of the
vine image in connection with the Eucharist. Sirach 24:17-21
compares wisdom to a vine that people eat. Thus the original
setting of the discourse—or of at least the first half of it—
may have been eucharistic.

John 15:1-6 *The True Vine*

Verses 1-2 are a short parable that begins with an I-Am
saying: "I am the true vine." The adjective true occurs in

4:23 and 6:32 as a polemic against Jewish images of salvation. Similar polemics are implied when Christians are understood as the true vineyard, to replace Israel (Mk 12:1–11
parr.). John may intend "true" to imply a contrast with
the unproductive vine, Israel, which still survives in the
synagogue, which will persecute the Christians (16:2). The
first analogy is that of pruning (cp. Jer 5:10, Ez 17:7).
Before the instrusion of v 3, the image does not seem to
have been negative. Rather, pruning was the activity of the
vine-dresser to guarantee the desired harvest.

Verse 3, an aside, breaks into the image to reassure the
disciples. The comment may refer back to 13:10b. A saying
such as that in 6:63—Jesus' words are spirit and life—may
lie behind this expression. The verse may have been added
to the discourse when it was put into the gospel (Brown,
2:676), or it may be a marginal gloss that was later copied
into the text.

Verse 4 connects the image of the fruit-bearing vine to the
community. Its exhortation to remain in Jesus recalls the
special relationship of Jesus and the Father and the community, described earlier (14:10f., 20; cf. 17:21, 23, 26). The
Evangelist does not clarify what is meant by bearing fruit.
John 4:36 and 12:24 connect it with missionary activity, but
later associations with the love command may indicate that
the author has the larger context of the Christian life in
mind.

Verse 5 repeats the opening I-Am saying, adding the
disciples as branches. This addition enables the Evangelist
to shift the analogy to the fate of the branches. The expression "you can do nothing without me" became a proof text
in later debates about the necessity of grace. The Johannine
saying goes back to earlier ones about the agent relationship between the Son and the Father: The Son does nothing
except what he "sees" the Father doing. As Jesus' agents,

Christians depend upon him for their mission, for bearing fruit.

Verse 6 accentuates the seriousness of the injunction to remain in Jesus with a new image: unprofitable branches being burned (cf. Ez 15:4-6, 19:12, Is 40:8). The verse seems to be an adaptation of a traditional Christian-judgment saying such as is found in Mt 3:10 or 13:30, since neither the language nor the form of the second part is typical of Johannine discourse.

John 15:7-17 *Remaining in Jesus and the Love Command*

The interpretations of the command to remain in Jesus recall many themes from the previous discourse: The Father is glorified; the love command establishes the new community; a new relationship is established between Jesus and his disciples; the disciples are assured that their prayer is answered. The passage is a collage of short sayings on these subjects, held together by catchwords.

The promise that prayer will be answered (vv. 7, 16) occurs in all the discourses. The Evangelist associates it with language about the disciples' mission and the glorification of the Father (vv. 8, 16; cp. 14:13). Just as he had portrayed Jesus as one whose unity with the Father meant that his prayer was always heard, the disciples now may have similar confidence that God will provide whatever is necessary for them to carry out their mission.

Verses 9-10 reiterate the theme that the love command, which is the identifying mark of the new community (cf. 13:34, 14:15, 21, 23), implies a new relationship between the Father, Jesus, and the disciples.

Verse 11 is a transitional verse, typical of John (cp. 14:25). Such expressions as "these things I have said" frequently introduce reasons for speaking (e.g., 14:29, so that the disciples will believe). The joy the disciples are to have (cp. 14:28) is clearly the eschatological joy predicted in the prophets (Is 25:9, 61:10, Zec 9:9f; cf Jn 3:29). It forms a key motif in the next discourse.

Verses 12-13 return to the love command (13:34). They present Jesus' death as the supreme example of what he meant.

Friendship with Jesus

Sayings about laying down one's life for friends occur in Hellenistic ethical teaching, where friendship between those who are equal in virtue was considered the noblest example of love. Jewish literature applied such language to the wise man. Wisdom was said to make people friends of God (Wis 7:27). Following Ex 33:11, the Jewish philosopher, Philo, presents Moses as such a friend of God, with whom he could speak openly (*heres.* 21; cp. *leg all.* iii.1).

Luke 12:4 is the only non-Johannine passage to speak of the disciples as Jesus' friends. John has already introduced the friendship motif in the Lazarus story (11:3, 11, 16). Verses 13-15 are his interpretation of the friendship tradition. Those who do what Jesus has commanded may be called friends. The slave/friend contrast in verse 15 may refer back to the slave/free contrast in 8:32-36. The slave/master contrast was part of the commissioning language in 13:16. Philosophical discussions of friendship held that the only true friendship is between virtuous people who are equals. The basis of "equality" for Christians is the perfection with which Jesus has carried out his mission: He has made known to the disciples everything he heard from the Father. Jesus' revelation, then, is what makes the disciples "friends." They must, of course, keep the commandments that are part of that revelation. But contrary to the philosophical accounts, they are not friends of Jesus because they have attained some equality with him in virtue. That point is brought home in the following verse, which returns to the commissioning language. They did not choose Jesus; he chose them. He has commissioned them to bear fruit.

The Johannine language about the divinity of Jesus is so pronounced that some find him somewhat inhuman. We should perhaps remember that this picture did not prevent the Johannine community from speaking of its relationship with Jesus as one of friendship.

Verse 17 closes the section with another statement of the love command.

John 15:18–16:4a *Hatred by the World*

The conclusion turns from the positive images of cohesion, fruitfulness, and love, which characterize the community, to the hostility and rejection that will be its lot in the world. Matthew 10:17–25 contains similar predictions that Christians will have to expect hostility and rejection for their preaching. Both passages suppose that the disciple is called upon to share the rejection and hatred which had been shown Jesus (v. 18; cp. Mt 10:22f.). Verses 19 formulates the opposition between the disciple and the world in Johannine symbols. Because they believe in Jesus, the disciples no longer belong to the world. Verse 20 quotes the commissioning language of 13:16. Since the disciples are now Jesus' agents, their word will have the same effect as his (20c; cp. Mt 10:14, 40). And, like that of Jesus, the rejection of the disciples proves that those who do such things do not know God (v. 21; cp. 5:36, 7:28, 8:19). Since knowing God implies keeping his commandments, it follows that those who reject his spokes-men are guilty of sin (vv. 22–24). Similar charges, that rejection of Jesus is sinful, rang through the controversy discourses. Psalm 69:5 is not used elsewhere in the NT to explain the rejection of Jesus, but the psalm is common in passion apologetic (Mk 15:36, Mt 27:34, Jn 19:29).

Matthew 10:20 (cp. Mk 13:9, 11) promised that the Spirit would aid the disciples when they have to stand trial for their faith. Verses 26–27 associate a similar promise with the Paraclete.

John 16:1–4a concludes the section with a final prediction of the trials to come, so that the disciples' faith will not be shaken (cp. Mk 14:27). We can learn from Paul's career that persecution of Christians was seen by some as a religious duty. The Evangelist warns of such persecutions, probably involved the kind of tough arguments against Christianity that form such a large part of the controversy stories in the gospel. In such circumstances, the disciples must not lose their faith (v. 4a).

The picture of hostility which this discourse presents throws the opening metaphor of unity and cohesion into a stronger light. The injunction to "remain in Jesus" could be taken as an exhortation to stay a Christian and not be discouraged by polemic and persecution—or, worse, return to Judaism. If they remain faithful, Christians can expect to be "friends of Jesus," just as much as Moses was "friend of God."

16. Sorrow Turns into Joy

Extensive duplications between chapters 14 and 16 (see the chart in Brown, 2: 589–93) suggest that we have two versions of the same themes. Brown (2:588) outlines a common structure: (1) Jesus' imminent departure, (2) question about where Jesus is going and sorrow of the disciples, (3) two Paraclete sayings, (4) disciples will see Jesus again, (5) Father loves the disciples, (6) answered prayer, and (7) disciples will desert Jesus during the passion.

The departure theme is much less theologically elaborate in this chapter than it was in chapter 14. It lacks both the indwelling language and the love command, which are common to the other discourses. Its Paraclete sayings are much closer to Jewish models than those in chapter 14. Since the love command is the key to the community's self-understanding, both in the other discourses and in the first epistle of John, it is hard to see how this chapter could have been composed by a later disciple of the Evangelist. Rather, we suggest that it is an earlier treatment of themes that the Evangelist used in chapter 14. This chapter picks up the departure/return theme, which was absent from chapter 15. The first section (vv. 4b–15) uses two Paraclete sayings to describe the consequences of Jesus' departure. The rest points out the sorrow/joy of the disciples that is to come from the departure/return of Jesus.

John 16:4b–6 *Introduction*

References to things Jesus has said are transitional (14:25, 16:1, 4, 6, 33). The first sentence suggests that Jesus' departure necessitates some "new" teaching that had not been presented during the life of Jesus. A similar statement occurs at the end of the discourse, where Jesus says that he had been speaking in figures but would soon speak plainly. Such references may allude to the creative "remembering" that occurred after Jesus' resurrection.

Verse 5 creates problems for any theory that would see all the discourses as composed at the same time. Jesus has been asked where he is going (13:36, 14:4f.), yet this version pays no attention to that discussion. It focuses on the grief of the disciples (cp. 14:27). The word for grief (*lupe*) occurs only here in the gospel. It seems to be equivalent to the eschatological term tribulation, used in 16:33—an allusion to the persecutions of the previous chapter?

John 16:7–11 *The Paraclete Condemns the World*

A solemn opening gives the promise of the Paraclete a revelatory character. The only other occurrence of the expression "it is beneficial for you" occurs in Caiaphas' prophecy (11:50, 18:14). That expression also adds to the solemnity of the pronouncement.

The benefits attributed to Jesus' crucifixion in the various passion predictions have all been announced as fulfilled in the earlier discourses. It will bestow life (3:14f.); Jesus' indwelling means that both he and they live (14:19). The world will know I-Am (8:28); the disciples will come to this knowledge (14:8–13). Jesus will draw all to himself (12:32); this is to be accomplished by the mission of the disciples. Here the benefit ascribed to Jesus' departure is the condemnation of the world that results from the Paraclete's coming. This passage uses the legal and forensic metaphors that have been used throughout the gospel. The legal process would not be complete if Jesus' departure had not led to the world's condemnation for disbelief. John does not project some apocalyptic vindication of Jesus in the future (cf. Schnackenburg, 3:148).

Formal sentence is passed against the world on three counts (v. 8), and each is taken up in the following verses. The Greek verb *elegchein* can be used in a technical, forensic sense to mean "convict" or, in a more general sense, "convince." John always uses the verb in a legal context (3:20, 8:46); so we accept the forensic translation, "convict." The term Paraclete (see the section "Paraclete") can also be a legal term for a defense attorney, and was so applied to Moses. Here it is reversed and used with the connotation of "prosecutor." A similar statement was made about Moses in 5:45: he will accuse the Jews rather than defend them.

The first count in the indictment is sin, that is, not believing in Jesus. A similar combination is made several times in the polemic of the gospel (8:21-24, 34-47, 9:39-41, 3:18, 36, 12:48, 15:4f.). Refusal to believe is the standard Johannine definition of sin. The next two charges also occur in contexts associated with this charge.

"Righteousness" occurs only in Jn 16:10, so its meaning must be determined from the grounds given. The controversy stories in 7:32-36 and 8:14-21 play on the theme that Jesus' departure will mean condemnation for those who cannot know where he is going. Jesus' knowledge of his origin and destiny is evidence for the truth of his testimony (8:14). Because the Jews do not know where he is going (i.e., back to God), they will die in their sin (8:21). The second-person plural, "and you [pl.] will no longer see me," cannot, in light of these parallels, refer to the disciples (cp. 8:21, 12:36b, 17:34). It must refer to nonbelievers, the "you" of the earlier controversies. Both discourses had questioned the judgment which nonbelievers make about Jesus (8:14). In 7:24, Jesus concludes his defense against charges of breaking the law with: "Do not judge according to appearances but judge according to just (*dikan*) judgment." The expression "just judgment" there seems to be equivalent to "righteousness" here. It refers specifically to false judgments about Jesus by those who fail to recognize his divine origin.

Verse 11 adds a further judgment against the ruler of the world (cf. 12:31). The controversy in chapter 8 reached its climax with the statement that the Devil is the father of Jesus' opponents. Here, condemnation of negative judgments about Jesus also ends with a cosmic statement. Jesus has triumphed over the ruler of the world. Satan's condemnation is not deferred until the parousia. Such an assertion is not merely "demythologizing" a story about the end of the world, it has important consequences for one's understanding of the salvation "delivered" by Jesus. Traditional Christian apocalyptic language could be said to leave salvation unfinished: As long as Satan has not been defeated, evil could be said to predominate in the "present evil age." A person might well have wondered whether Jesus would ever get around to fulfilling the messianic promises. Perhaps other messiahs or prophets would be necessary? John's statement claims that the final victory has already been won. Not only is the world wrong about Jesus, but even about its own ruler.

With its references to the terminology of the controversy stories, this section insists upon the truth of Christian claims for Jesus against the challenges that were launched by his detractors. Not only does it answer the hostilities and controversies of the earlier chapters, it must also answer the one trial yet to come, the passion.

John 16:12–15 *The Spirit of Truth as Guide*

The introduction to the second Paraclete saying resembles

verse **4b**. Unlike 14:25, which limits the Paraclete's activity to "remembering," both these introductions suggest that there is to be more to what the Paraclete teaches than what the disciples have heard during the lifetime of Jesus. The disciples' inability to bear Jesus' words intensifies the motif of grief. The spirit-of-Truth figure has been assimilated to the agency language of the gospel (vv. 14f.). Perhaps an earlier saying about the Spirit of Truth has been reformulated.

In verse 13, "that one" refers to the "that one comes" of verse 8. John uses such expressions as "into all truth" with varying degrees of theological significance. In 4:23f, it is merely adverbial, whereas in 8:44 the fact that the Devil does not stand "in truth" indicates his essential opposition to Jesus. Perhaps the closest parallel occurs in 17:15-19, where Jesus asks the Father to sanctify the disciples "in truth" (= his word). Truth establishes the disciples in a hostile world. John 8:31-47 connects remaining in Jesus' word and knowing the truth. Perhaps this question of fidelity to Jesus' word (cf. 15:3, 20) is what the Evangelist means by the promise that the Spirit will lead the disciples into all truth. In that case, this expression is the antithesis to the things the disciples cannot bear.

Verse 13b places the Spirit in the same context as Jesus' teaching. Only those who do not speak "on their own" speak truth. Caiaphas did not speak "on his own" when he prophesied correctly about Jesus' death (11:51). Jesus never speaks "on his own." Everything he teaches is from the Father (cf. 5:19, 7:18, 12:49, 14:10).

The promise that the Spirit will announce "things to come" causes difficulty because it is not clear what is being referred to. In Jewish literature, the expression referred to the events of the end of the world. These were explained to the seer by God or an angel. The Essenes thought that the person who founded their sect had taught the proper eschatological interpretation of OT prophecies: they referred to the history of the sect and the events of the end-time. Their commentary on Habkakuk says of that prophet: "God told him to write down *the things that were to come,* but He did not tell him when that moment would come to fulfillment" (I QpHab vii.1ff.). The Essenes thought that those prophecies were being fulfilled in their own time. They also use the expression "Spirit of Truth," usually to refer to the Spirit which guides the righteous (I QS iii.18ff., 24; iv.2).

We suggest that behind this Johannine passage lay an earlier tradition about the Spirit of Truth's announcing "things to come" to the Christians. The saying may well have understood their being led into all truth in a similar fashion. In such a saying, "things to come" would not refer to indefinite events in the future but to the eschatological interpretation of the OT, presumably to demonstrate that its promises have been fulfilled by Jesus.

The setting in which the Evangelist uses the saying gives it a different focus. Verses 12, 14, and 15 connect the Spirit's activity to the words of Jesus. The Spirit glorifies Jesus by leading the disciples to a true understanding of his teaching, just as Jesus' ministry has glorified the Father. The Evangelist returns to his agent metaphor to clarify what the Spirit reveals. Jesus, as agent, had received everything from the Father who sent him. The Paraclete only passes on revelation he receives from Jesus; it would not be possible for him to reveal something new, even from the Father. Everything has been included in Jesus' revelation.

John 16:16–24 *Seeing Jesus Again*

As in chapter 14, the announcement of Jesus' departure leads to perplexity among the disciples; here they question each other, rather than Jesus. The Evangelist frequently had

Jesus answer questions that were being discussed by others, which were not addressed directly to him (e.g., 2:24f., 5:17, 6:43, 7:28). The disciples question both the statement in verse 16 and the "I am going to the Father" of verse 5, but the focus of the answer is on the "little while," when the disciples do not see Jesus and mourn and then see him and rejoice (v. 19). Some interpreters suppose that "little while" refers to the time between the crucifixion and the resurrection, but when John speaks of "seeing Jesus again" he has more than Easter in mind. Jesus' new presence is permanent (vv. 22f.).

Jesus' explanation contrasts the joy of the world with the sorrow of the disciples. The image of a woman in labor was used to explain the sufferings that must come before the joy of the messianic age (Is 26:17–18, 66:7–10; cp. Mk 13:19, 24). John declared that the judgment of the ruler of the world—who is ultimately responsible for those sufferings—has taken place (16:11) with the coming of the Paraclete. He could hardly be allowed to bring further apocalyptic woes upon the disciples. Instead, those trials are seen to have been undergone by the disciples after the crucifixion. With Jesus' return, they attain the true eschatological joy, which no one can take away (v. 22).

The Presence of Salvation

The Johannine reinterpretation of eschatological language has profound significance for the situation in which the community finds itself. The fantastic symbols and mythic language of apocalyptic project an image of a time in the future, when salvation will be assured and revelation complete. Sin, death, and disease will finally be eradicated and the cosmos will be as God intended. Before that happens, God's purposes are at least partially obscured, if not obstructed, by the presence of evil. By transposing such language to the ministry of Jesus and the experience of the disciples, the Evangelist shows an immense confidence in the presence of salvation (a confidence with some parallels in the kingdom preaching of Jesus). It becomes possible to deny that whole understanding of the world which sees it as subject to a variety of evil powers—an understanding that has its contemporary analogies. John does not deny that there is sin, death, and evil in the world; the experiences of his community are proof enough of that. But these experiences are no more proof that evil dominates the world than is the death of Jesus. (Nor do they prove that the world is ontologically evil, as the Gnostics believed.) They only show that, for a variety of reasons, some people do not "know God."

The Christian is not to worry about "making it through" tribulations and evil times to get to life, salvation, and joy in some future time or place. He or she has all of this through his or her experience of Jesus. In short, the believer relates to his or her world in terms of what he or she has, rather than in terms of what is expected for the future. To abandon Christianity under persecution, then, would be to abandon a present and sure salvation—not simply to change one's expectations about the future.

The promises in verses 23-24 continue this language of a certain, sure salvation. The disciple will finally understand Jesus' revelation (v. 23a), and he or she may be confident that God answers prayer (vv. 23b, 24).

John 16:25-33 *Speaking Plainly about the Father*

"These things I have said . . ." introduces the conclusion to the discourse. Jesus says he has been speaking in figures but will now speak plainly. The contrast reminds us of the two levels on which Jesus' words have been read throughout the gospel. On the literal level, they are perplexing, if not contradictory. They make sense only to the believer who knows the salvation about which Jesus speaks. We have also been told, several times, that the disciples did not understand things Jesus did until after the resurrection. Here it is the Father about whom Jesus will speak openly. In the Fourth Gospel, the crucifixion is the "open" revelation of the Father. The passion prediction at 8:28 says that the crucifixion would manifest Jesus' divine I AM; Jn 14:31 that the crucifixion would show that Jesus loves the Father and does everything he commands. The crucifixion is portrayed as the time of the mutual glorification of Father and Son (13:31ff.). The Evangelist may have all these points in mind when he says that Jesus is about to speak openly of the Father.

Verses 26 repeats the promise that prayer will be answered (cp. 23b–24). Jesus grounds that promise in the new relationship between God and the disciples. He (the Father) loves those who believe in Jesus (v. 27; cp. 17:21–26). The verb that is used for "love" is cognate with the Greek word for friend, used in 15:15, where friendship is the new relationship between Jesus and the disciples. It may be (Schnackenburg, 3:184) that we have more of the Johannine reinterpretation of Hellenistic friendship language. Because they believe, the disciples become friends of God. Therefore, this tradition may also supply the key to what is meant by "speaking plainly" (clearly, directly). Philo used the same word to describe Moses as the one who speaks to God directly, as to a friend. One of Moses' functions was to intercede for Israel, the saying about prayer in verse 26 has cast Jesus in that role. Therefore we suggest that verses 25–27 are allusions to the Johannine reinterpretation of the tradition about Moses as friend of God. Through Jesus, the believer now has that kind of direct relationship to God which people had formerly thought belonged to Moses. (This reinterpretation was probably part of the larger view of the Mosaic tradition, such as turning him into the accuser of Israel.)

Verse 28 summarizes the career of Jesus as it has been presented in the gospel: He came into the world from the Father; now he is leaving to return to the Father (cp. 17:4ff; this sentence also answers the question implied in verses 5, 17). The disciples take this statement of Jesus' origin and destination as an indication that the time of clear speaking and understanding has come (v. 29b). They make a correct confession of faith: Jesus is from God. But their actions when the hour comes will show that they have not understood what Jesus has been telling them. They have not been through their hour of grief and tribulation.

John 16:32 uses Zec 13:7 to suggest that the disciples will desert Jesus in his hour. Although the gospel does not have a scene in which they do so, the flight of the disciples occurs in other passion accounts (cf. Mk 14:27, 50). The presence of the beloved disciple at the cross (19:20) and of the disciples in Jerusalem (20:19) seem to contradict this tradition. This particular piece of tradition was probably part of the pre-Johannine passion account. But, throughout the gospel, the Evangelist is careful to emphasize the fact that the passion does not mean that God has abandoned him; so he points out that Jesus was not left alone—God was with him.

Verse 33 may be said to express the purpose of this discourse. Despite the tribulations they must undergo in the world, the disciples have peace in Christ (cp. 14:27). Jesus' victory over the world (cp. 14:30, 16:11) has guaranteed their salvation and the permanent joy that they will possess.

The Paraclete

Extensive debate rages around the five Paraclete sayings

in the gospel. The discussion is still a long way from any consensus; so we can only present what seem to us the main lines of a plausible solution to the problems presented by these sayings. Difficulties lie in three main areas: (a) the background and origin of the term paraclete, (b) the literary status of the five passages, and (c) the theological significance of the sayings. The reader may find further discussion of the debate in the commentaries (Brown, 2: 1135–44; Schnackenburg, 3: 156–73).

Background

The term paraclete occurs only in the NT in the Johannine literature. 1 John 2:1ff. speaks of the exalted Jesus as "our Paraclete" (= intercessor, advocate), and the word is used in its usual secular sense; it is not a title. It probably represents the transfer to Jesus of the picture of Moses as the heavenly intercessor for Israel that can be found in every sector of Judaism (see Meeks, *Prophet-King* pp, 118–254). The Johannine community clearly considered Jesus superior to Moses (1:17f.) and could easily have given him the intercessor role. But the Paraclete image in the gospel is not that of a heavenly defense attorney; so it cannot be a direct appropriation of that Mosaic tradition.

Since there is no definite Paraclete figure in other literature that answers to the variety of functions given the Paraclete in the gospel, most interpreters suggest that the Evangelist has put together a variety of images. Brown's proposal is typical of such a solution: a combination of OT materials, late Jewish angelology, and early Christian traditions lies behind these passages.

(a) *OT Traditions:* Brown invokes the tandem relationship between a figure and his successor to explain the image (e.g., Moses/Joshua, Dt 34:9; Elijah/Elisha, 2 Kgs 2:9, 15).

The "second person" has characteristics of the one he follows. Brown argues that the Paraclete is closely modeled on Jesus: He comes as Jesus did; is called "another" Paraclete, implying that Jesus was the first; has a similar relationship to the disciples and to the world (Brown, 2:1140–41).

Some of the passages that are cited to prove these points are tenuous. The real parallels between the relationship of the Paraclete and of Jesus to the disciples are between the Paraclete and the heavenly Jesus, not the earthly one he is said to follow in the tandem theory. However, Brown is surely correct to have pointed out the importance of successor relationships in these sayings. We have seen that Jesus has commissioned the disciples as his agents. The Paraclete is to assist them in that witness.

(b) *Late Jewish Angelology:* Because the Paraclete is called Spirit of Truth, interpreters suggest that late Jewish angelology played a role in forming this picture. The Qumran texts speak of a Prince of Light, and Angel of Truth, who guides the righteous against those who belong to the Prince of Darkness, Satan (I QS iii.18–24; I QM xiii.9–12). They also speak of a spirit of truth, which guides people (I QS iv.2, 21; T Jud xx.1–5), but this spirit is not an angel. It guides the righteous to choose the works of God rather than those of Satan. Like a conscience, it will condemn each person at the judgement of the evil he has done. John may have derived Spirit of Truth from such traditions as our study of 16:13 indicated, but the Paraclete does not correspond to such an angelic figure.

(c) *Early Christian Traditions:* Traditions about the Holy Spirit are often suggested as a source of the Paraclete traditions (cf. Dodd, *Hist. Trad,* pp. 410–13). John 14:26 calls the Paraclete "Holy Spirit." Some of his functions, such as helping the disciples bear witness to Jesus, are closely related to synoptic sayings about the Spirit (15:26; cp. Mt 10:20,

Acts 6:10). In other places, the Spirit is clearly distinct from the Paraclete figure, as in the association between the Spirit and baptism (3:5) or the Spirit as Jesus' eschatological gift to the believer (7:38).

Since none of these sources provides an exact parallel to the Johannine material, we must assume that the traditions to which the author refers were formulated within the Johannine community. As with its symbols, the Fourth Gospel never uses a tradition in a completely conventional manner.

Literary Analysis

Further understanding of the process by which the Johannine community came to this rather unusual symbol depends upon literary analysis of the passages. One's understanding of the literary history of this section of the gospel, and of the sayings in particular, determines the stage at which particular views entered the Johannine tradition. Some argue that all the Paraclete sayings were inserted into the discourses by a redactor, others that they are an integral part of the chapters in which they occur. But chapters 15–17 are often held to have been composed at different times, either by the Evangelist himself or by a disciple(s) who used chapter 14 as a model. Frequently, whatever theory an author holds, he or she treats all five sayings as though they form a harmonious group and reflect the same view (cf. Brown, 2: 581–84).

Comparison of the various sayings shows that those in chapter 14 are quite different from those in chapter 16. Those in chapter 14 are clearly internalized and seem to represent an alternative formulation of the indwelling language used in that chapter. The Paraclete *remains* with the disciples, as Jesus does, and solves the riddling misunderstandings that are characteristic of the Johannine style. The language of chapter 16 fits in more directly with other Johannine metaphors: 16:7ff. is forensic, part of the whole complex of judgment metaphors used in the gospel; 16:11ff. is close to traditional language of prophecy and eschatological interpretation.

The sayings are structured as follows:

14:16: Father (at Jesus' request) sends Paraclete to disciples.

14:26: Father (in Jesus' name) sends Paraclete to disciples. Both sayings are identical in structure; both restrict the Paraclete's activity to remaining with the disciples and leading them to understand the teaching of Jesus.

15:26: Jesus sends Paraclete (from Father) to disciples as witness to Jesus before the world. The locus of the Paraclete's activity is not within the Christian community but in the witness that the Christian must bear before the world.

16:7ff: Jesus sends Paraclete to the disciples to convict the world.

16:13: Spirit of Truth (from Jesus, v. 14; from Father, v. 15) comes to disciples. The first saying in chapter 16 employs the language of judgment, and the Paraclete's primary function pertains to the world. The second (see commentary on 16:13) uses an eschatological saying about interpretation of prophecies of the end. Thus both are reinterpretations of eschatological language.

The legal meaning of "paraclete," defense attorney, would seem appropriate for the eschatological, judgment sayings of chapter 16. But the legal image in 16:7ff. clearly casts the Paraclete as prosecutor of Jesus' case against the world. A similar reversal occurs at 5:45: Moses, the defense attorney of the Jews, will become their accuser. In Jewish sources, Moses as defense attorney could be spoken of as "paraclete.'' The Evangelist is clearly the one responsible for this reversal. We suggest that the Evangelist has done the same thing in 16:7ff.: The defender will convict those who do not believe in Jesus. This is probably one of a number of such reversals. They were probably slogans that were formulated during the Johannine community's debate with Judaism: Moses will accuse the Jews before God (ch. 5); Satan, not Abraham, is the real father of the Jews (ch. 8); the defense counsel is a prosecuting attorney (ch. 16).

The Spirit of Truth may originally have been an independent figure, like the one at Qumran, who guided the community in its eschatological interpretation of Scripture. The Spirit of Truth and the Paraclete are only indirectly associated in chapter 16, whereas chapter 14 shows that they were eventually assimilated into one. Just as the Jewish *Testament of Judah* has taken the Spirit of Truth as an internal witness to a person's deeds, the association of the Paraclete and the Spirit of Truth enables one to see that the condemnation of the Jews/the world/nonbelievers, which the Johannine tradition expected, had already taken place within the community. The Evangelist then formulated the sayings in 14:16f; 26 that associate the two figures and locate the Paraclete's activity entirely within the Christian community. The forensic associations of the term are not evident in chapter 14. The identification of the two had become common enough for either to be used of the activity of the Spirit within the community.

Theological Significance

The significance attributed to the Paraclete traditions usually depends upon whether a commentator takes the forensic or the guidance sayings as the primary meaning of the whole group. Focus on the activity within the community invites comparison with other NT traditions about the Spirit. They clearly promise guidance—even inerrancy?—to the community in its understanding of what has been revealed. Some commentators have even suggested that this belief is the source of the Evangelist's confidence in his reinterpretation.

Attention to the forensic connotations of "paraclete" has led to a variety of interpretations in which the believer is the final recipient of such testimony. His or her questions are overcome. Bultmann, for example, takes all the sayings to refer to a single, inner event:

> But the one event that is meant by all these sayings is not an external occurrence but an inner one: the victory which Jesus wins when faith arises in man by the overcoming of the offense which Jesus is to him. The victory over the ruler of the world which Jesus has won is the fact that now there exists a faith which recognizes in Jesus the revelation of God [NT Theol., 2:57].

While Bultmann is surely correct to insist on looking for the theological significance of the forensic sayings, we find two points in this interpretation objectionable. First, the reduction of all the Paraclete sayings to a single mold glosses over the two different theological traditions that have been employed in their formulation. Second, we suggest that, throughout the discourse, the Evangelist is speaking of the community and its experience of presence, not of individuals.

People often have difficulty remembering that the Bible speaks of salvation in terms of a community of the redeemed, the people of God. They tend to reduce all biblical language about salvation to individual salvation. The Church has been trying to correct this misapprehension by stressing the communal aspects of the sacraments, as the new rites for baptism and penance do so clearly. In recent years a number of fields of study have been stressing how much a person's character and experience owe to the society and communities in which he or she lives. Such awareness is behind the attempts of many Christian communities to restructure and revitalize their sense of the Church as a community of believers. At the same time, we must be careful not to lose the cutting edge of the Christian message. Although we may not feel the necessity to speak a language of opposition and hostility to the world, such as that employed in this gospel, we should not allow the privileged and familiar status of Christianity to blunt its critical effect. Jesus must still be a scandalous and perplexing figure. We have plenty critics of our own—even some who would be quite willing to see Jesus as a "great man" but are quite unable to make any sense of claims that he is the final and definitive revelation of God. Many might hope for some future victory over evil, but few have "the gall" to proclaim that Jesus has already won such a victory.

But these claims by the forensic Paraclete sayings are not the only difficult ones. Those about the Spirit's guidance of the community are even more puzzling, especially in an age of general skepticism about human institutions. Should such a promise be limited solely to the magisterium of the Roman Catholic or some other denomination? Or must some broader and more ecumenical view of the inerrancy of the Church be found? We cannot attempt an answer to these theological questions here; they require the work of historical and systematic theology for their solution. But the Evangelist insists that Christian theology must include some understanding of the finality of God's revelation in Jesus, of the uniqueness of his salvation, of Jesus' victory over evil, and of the accurate preservation of his teaching within the Christian community.

17. Jesus' Prayer for His Disciples

The final section of the discourse material is a lengthy prayer. There is no exact parallel to this type of prayer in literature that is contemporary with the Fourth Gospel. Jewish testament literature often concludes with a prayer in which the patriarch blesses his sons (cf. Dt 33, Moses; Jub 10:3-6, Noah). The language of the Johannine prayer: praise to God and prayer/enlightenment for those a departing revealer leaves behind, is closer to the type of prayer which concludes some Hermetic writings (CH I, 31-32; XIII, 21-22). Although the prayer contains liturgical language (e.g., v. 11, "holy Father"), it does not follow any known liturgical models. It is dominated by the language of Johannine Christology. Like the shorter prayers in the gospel, this one is more a statement of the unity between Jesus and the Father, which validates his mission, than a petition. One may view it as the culmination of the language about unity which has occurred throughout the gospel. Jesus now speaks as one who has completed his mission and who leaves the community to continue his testimony to the world.

Several proposals about the structure of the prayer have been advanced. Since we take verses 1-5 as an introduction modeled on 13:31f, we see the whole prayer as focused on the disciples. Therefore we do not follow Brown's division of the prayer into three parts, with verses 1-8 as Jesus' prayer for his own glorification (Brown, 2:749). Schnackenburg (3:191) makes the interesting suggestion that the prayer should be divided into six sections, on stylistic grounds. We suggest a slightly different structure: (1) verses 1-5, Jesus' return to glory; (2) verses 6-11a, Jesus' mission accomplished with the commissioning of the disciples; (3) verses 11b-23, three prayers for the newly commissioned; (4) verses 24–26, conclusion, the destiny of the disciples.

Although this prayer came to be called the "high priestly prayer of Jesus," it does not use priestly imagery. Rather, it is a triumphant statement that the divine Word returns to the Father with his mission accomplished. At the same time, the believers who are left behind are encouraged to continue with the mission for which they have been sent.

John 17:1–5 *The Hour of Jesus' Glorification*

These verses resemble the introduction to the first discourse (13:31f.). The hour for Jesus' glorification has now come. His mission has glorified the Father; he, in turn, will be glorified. This prayer points out other connections that were only implied in the earlier passage. Jesus is returning to the glory he had before creation. We are thus reminded of the gospel's opening hymn (1:5, 14; cp. Phil 2:6–11, Heb 1:3). Jesus as divine Word has authority over the whole world (v. 2; cp. Mt 28:18, where that authority is given to the risen Lord). Jesus' authority/glory is active in the world in his gift of eternal life (v. 2; cp. 1:4).

The parenthetical insertion of verse 3 clarifies what is meant by eternal life. The verse is in the form of a short creedal statement, possibly derived from the liturgy of the Johannine Church. Knowledge of "the one true God" is an assertion of monotheism that is typical of early Christian preaching to the Gentiles (cf. Acts 17:24). The second item of belief is that Jesus is the one sent by God. The gospel has spelled out the implications of that statement: Jesus is the only way to, that is, revelation of God. These introductory verses, then, return to themes from the prologue to place the mission of Jesus back in a universal context. Jesus has accomplished the life-giving mission of the divine Word.

John 17:6–11a *The Completion of Jesus' Mission*

These verses detail the completion of Jesus' mission. Obviously, the entire universe did not respond to the revetion; that was stated from the beginning (1:11). Rather, the fulfillment of that mission lay in the creation of a believing community (1:12). The Evangelist piles up the metaphors he has been using for accepting Jesus as the revelation of the Father: "Keep his word"; "know that Jesus is from the Father." These expressions have pointed out the uniqueness of Jesus as revealer. "Making known the name of God" is OT language for making known his salvation (Is 52: 5f, Ez 39:7). John understands the Is 52:5 text to mean that salvation is shown in a special name, the divine I AM (see Brown, 2:756). Jesus identified himself with that name and promised that his glorification would make it manifest to the world (8:29). But the future of that revelation in the world depends upon the community of believers Jesus leaves behind. They are the ones for whom he now prays (vv. 9f.).

Commentators have made much of the expression "I am no longer in the world" (v. 11). Some have claimed that it shows the entire prayer was understood to have been spoken by the risen/glorified Jesus (contrary to v. 13). This passage is shot through with the language that John has consistently used to speak of Jesus as the one sent by the Father. Everything the disciples are said to know/believe belongs to that context. But the presupposition of all the discourses in this section of the gospel is that Jesus transfers the task of being God's witnesses in the world to the community of believers. They are to be his agents; through them, he (and the Father) is glorified. Jesus' work must end with the commissioning of those who will represent him. Verse 11, then, formulates that conviction in a new way. Jesus is no longer in the world, because his mission of testimony to unbelievers is concluded, and that of the disciples is just beginning.

John 17:11b-23 *Prayers for Those Commissioned*

Three prayers express what is necessary for the disciples to carry out their mission. The various controversy stories and the prediction of the world's hatred (15:18–16:4a) have acquainted us with the difficulties that face the Johannine community. These prayers are not just pious sentiments; they reflect the struggle of the community to maintain its faith and its conviction that its mission rests on the same divine sanction as that of Jesus.

(a) *Verses 11b-16:* The expression "holy Father" in 11b may be derived from liturgical usage (cp. Did 10:2). First, Jesus asks that the disciples be kept in the name which the Father has given him. That name may be the divine I AM. If so, the unity of the disciples is predicated on recognition of Jesus' divine identity. This prayer recalls injunctions to "remain in" Jesus, voiced in chapter 15 (cf. 15:6f.). The gospel never hints at internal threats to the unity of the Church, though the Johannine epistles suggest that such threats arose later. Therefore it seems more likely that the appeal for unity is a reflection of external threats. At the same time, unity is an important symbol in the gospel. The final justification of Jesus' mission and his claim to be the only way to salvation is his unity with the Father. That justification is now extended to the community.

Verse 12 contrasts the disciples' new situation with the situation when Jesus was active in his ministry. As an exhortation, it suggests that their situation should be no different than when he was among them. Jesus has lost nothing of what was entrusted to him by the Father (cp. 10:28a). Judas' failure was predicted, though the Evangelist does not give the exact place here (cf. 13:18).

Previous discourses also spoke of the joy which was to come to the disciples (15:11, 16:20, 22, 24). Like chapter 15, this passage also contrasts the joy of the disciples with the hatred they encounter in the world (cp. 15:18–21). Both passages stress the fact that the disciples are not "from the world." John 15:19 made it clear that they are not "from the world," because Jesus has chosen them. They do not have that status because some ontological difference sets them apart from others or because of something they have done. It depends entirely upon Jesus' choice of the disciple.

Verse 15 is important for the community's self-understanding. Even though they are opposed to the world, the disciples are not taken out of it. Some interpreters have taken the hostility toward the world, reflected in the symbolism of these chapters, to indicate that the Johannine community was tending to become an esoteric sect. We suppose that this symbolism had exhortatory value. It enables the believers to hold to their faith in a difficult time by focusing on its divine sanction. But all the commissioning language of these chapters points out that they cannot be withdrawn from the world; they must bear the same witness to it as Jesus.

Jesus' prayer that they be kept from the evil one reminds us of the last petition of the Lord's Prayer in Mt 6:13b. Perhaps this petition and the address "Father," used in all the prayers in the gospel, as well as the "Father, glorify your name" of 12:28, are echoes of that prayer as it was known in the Johannine community. This expression also sets the hatred experienced by the disciples in the same cosmic context as the hatred against Jesus; it is the activity of Satan. But the believer need not fear such opposition; if Satan has no power over Jesus, he can have no power over him or her either. Verse 16 concludes the first prayer by repeating 14b.

(b) *Verses 17–19:* The second petition request sanctification for the disciples, who are being sent (v. 18). John 10:36 speaks of Jesus as having been sanctified and sent by the

Father. Here, the word of the Father, which Jesus has given them, sanctifies the disciples for their mission (cp. 15:3). Verse 19 links the sanctification of the disciples with Jesus' death. The preposition *hyper* (for the sake of) frequently occurs in sacrificial interpretations of the death of Jesus. John uses it in three contexts to describe the death of Jesus: the eucharistic formula (6:51b), the shepherd for the sheep (10:11, 15, 15:13), and Caiaphas' prophecy (11:50-52, 18:14). Throughout this passage the saving realities are mediated to the disciples by the actions of Jesus. This mediation again reminds us of one of the Evangelist's basic themes: Jesus is the only revelation of God; he is the only Savior; the only way to the Father. Thus any relationship the disciples have to the Father is through Jesus. His death has made that relationship possible, and his presence in the community continues it.

(c) *Verses 20-23:* These verses pick up the unity theme from 11b. Unity may be seen as the goal of the entire prayer. Schnackenburg (3:214f.) finds verses 20-21 repetitious and awkward, and thinks they were inserted by a redactor. However, the Evangelist frequently adds parenthetical remarks to clarify his meaning. These verses do just that. Someone might think that what Jesus has just said is applicable only to the disciples who are with him; however, the Evangelist makes sure that we understand that the whole community of believers at any time is meant. His teaching about the source and nature of the Church's mission is to be the permanent possession of the Christian community. These verses apply the same commissioning to later believers that the earlier verses applied to the disciples.

Verses 22-23 return to the general prayer—now that we understand that the whole applies to all believers. Jesus' gift of glory to the disciples refers back to his glorification of the Father (cp. 15:4). The expression "the glory you gave me I have given them so that they might be one as we are one" reminds us of 11b: "sanctify them in the name which you gave me so that they might be one as we are." The goal of all Jesus' gifts of salvation and revelation is the realization of the unity between himself and the Father, as reflected in the unity of the believers. Verse 23a establishes that unity on the indwelling which unites Jesus, the Father, and the disciples (cp. 14:20, 23). Verse 23b ties that unity to the witness which the disciples must bear (cp. 13:34, 14:23). The "world" must learn two things through that testimony: first, that Jesus is the one sent and loved by God and, second, that the disciples continue that relationship with the Father.

Unity

Many scholars point to the use of the word *yahad,* unity, in the rule at Qumran as background for the use of "unity" in John. The Essenes speak of one's joining their community as being gathered into, as becoming, a unity (I QS V 2, 7). In their rule, the term is interchangeable with "community." It encompasses their sense of being the elect, the holy remnant of Israel. Such language may have been known to and used by the Johannine community, but the Evangelist, clearly, has done more with the designation. He was assimilated it to the unity between sender and agent, which has expressed the relationship between Father and Son throughout the gospel. In the process—as with many of his metaphors—an image which originally applied to the chosen people has come to express the Christology of the Evangelist. Unity is no longer an independent property of the eschatological remnant.

This assimilation allows the Evangelist to attribute a deeper significance to unity, when applied to the community, than he could have attributed if he had retained the traditional metaphor. The unity of the community is founded in and testifies to the truth of his basic Christological insight: Jesus and the Father are one.

Such unity cannot be understood, then, as simply some spiritual insight about the foundation of the Church. Nor can it be created by or identified with merely human solidarity. It is a divine gift which the Evangelist sees as grounded in the faith and love of God held by believers. It presents its challenge to the world through their testimony to that faith and the love they show one another.

These brief reflections on unity may also direct our reflections on ecumenism. We often try to create unity through institutional manipulations—common prayers, common places and times of worship, or common social and educational endeavors. While these are all clearly necessary for the Church in our time, they should not obscure the deeper dimensions of Christian unity which the Evangelist outlines for us. Common belief in Jesus and genuine, mutual love among Christians are the real characteristics of Church unity. If we neglect these fundamental dimensions, ecumenism may be nothing more than a "second religion," to be added to or practiced along with our particular denominational commitments.

John 17:24-26 *The Destiny of Believers*

The prayer concludes with a vision of the true destiny that awaits believers. First, they are to be with Jesus and see his glory (v. 26; cp. 14:3). But, as with "dwellings" in 14:3, the Evangelist does not propose the future eschatological promise without a correlate in the present experience of the community. In chapter 14 that correlate was the indwelling of Father and Son; here it is the community's experience of the presence of Jesus and of God's love for them. Members of the community can be sure that the Father's love for them is identical with his love for Jesus. This love is the culmination of Jesus' mission from the Father (cp. 3:16).

PART FOUR

Crucifixion/Resurrection: The Glorification of Jesus

18. Arrest and Trial of Jesus

The differences between John's account of the passion and accounts in the other gospels again suggest that he has used an account similar to, but independent of, the synoptic tradition. He has reworked that account to highlight the theological significance of the events he narrates. His account will display Jesus' true authority and kingship, who is always in control of what happens. No one takes Jesus' life away from him (cf. 10:18).

John 18:1-11 *The Arrest of Jesus*

Unlike the synoptics, John has no agony scene. John 12:27 suggests that he knew of the agony of Jesus but has relocated it. The arrest is told in such a way as to stress Jesus' control over the events. The designation of the garden as a customary meeting place was probably traditional (cp. Lk 22:39). Identification of the two groups who come to arrest Jesus causes some difficulty. Servants of the high priest have been sent against Jesus before (7:32, 45). The other accounts have only Jewish police, but John includes a "cohort" commanded by a *chiliarch*—a group of Roman soldiers. Perhaps his source used the Greek terminology for Roman soldiers in a nontechnical sense to refer to the Jewish police, and the Evangelist then took it in the technical sense. The fact that Pilate is totally ignorant of who Jesus is and why he is brought before him (18:29) makes it difficult to suppose that the source had the Romans involved in the arrest. Also, John may have wished to include the Romans because he understands the trial and crucifixion to be Jesus' manifestation before the whole world. The parallel between Pharisees and chief priests is anachronistic; it represents the situation in John's time, when the Pharisees had becomes leaders of the Jews (cf. 7:32, 45; 11:47-51).

Jesus' control is emphasized. He knows what is about to happen (v. 4). Further, Judas does nothing to identify Jesus. Jesus himself asks the approaching squad whom they seek and he identifies himself (v. 5). The Evangelist understands Jesus' "I Am" as more than a self-identification; it is the divine name. When Jesus pronounces it, the soldiers fall to the ground as at an epiphany (v. 6). Jesus must repeat his question, "Whom do you seek?" for the story to continue. Thus it is made clear that Jesus could have avoided arrest if he had wanted to. The Evangelist never lets us forget that Jesus' death was voluntary, in fulfillment of the Father's plan—not a frustration of that plan or proof that Jesus' claims about his relationship to God were false.

Jesus then manifests his control over the events of his arrest by disposing of the fate of his disciples. (Similar concern will be manifested from the cross [19:26].) Jesus gives himself up freely and obtains the release of his disciples. He had prophesied that they would flee (16:33), but there is no account of their flight. Perhaps his words to the guard, that the disciples are to be freed, were originally an explanation of their flight. The Evangelist has given them a different significance, however; he refers to Jesus' earlier saying that none of those who were given to him would perish (10:28; cf. 6:39, 17:12). Jesus is demonstrating that he is the ideal shepherd by giving up his life while seeing that the disciples go free.

The second disciple incident—again, John's fondness for paired stories may have led him to create the scene with the guard—combines two pieces of tradition. First, a version of the legend that one of the disciples tried to fight for

Jesus (cf. Lk 22:50f.) has Peter named as the disciple and gives the slave a name; Malchus. Both will reappear in the denial scene. Compared with the famed willingness of Jewish freedom fighters to die rather than surrender to anyone, Jesus' disciples must have seemed somewhat cowardly to many people (though such violent action would have been contrary to what we know of Jesus' teaching). This story probably found its place in the tradition to explain that Jesus' disciples could or would have fought had their master not prevented it. Later, the scene is evidence that Jesus' kingship is not political (18:36).

Verse 11b brings in another passion tradition: drinking the cup given by the Father (Mk 14:36/Mt 26:24; cp. Mk 10:38./Mt 20:22f.). Usually part of the agony scene, here, like the earlier allusion to that scene (12:27), it expresses Jesus' complete willingness to accomplish the mission the Father has given him.

John 18:12–27 *Annas Interrogates Jesus, and Peter's Denial*

The accounts of Jesus' interrogation by Jewish authorities differ (see chart in Brown, 2:830f.). Quite unlike the others, John has no proceeding before the Sanhedrin. Jesus is interrogated by someone John knows is not even the high priest at the time, Annas (v. 13). Since Luke has an interrogation before the Sanhedrin but no trial, some scholars (see Brown, 2:832) suppose that Luke and John are evidence that the primitive passion account did not contain a formal trial by Jewish authorities. On the other hand, John may have omitted that trial because Jesus has been tried by Jewish authorities since chapter 5, where the formal charge of blasphemy is first brought against him. The trial scene in 7:45–52 rejected Jesus' claims to be the Messiah and hinted that he was liable to death as one who leads the people astray. Jesus has already been condemned by an earlier session of the Sanhedrin (11:47-52), and John reminds us of that session (v. 14). We know the Jews have sentenced Jesus.

Peter's Denial

The Evangelist frames the interrogation of Jesus with the story of Peter's denial. Thus, we see, two interrogations proceed simultaneously: Jesus insisting on the truth of his mission, Peter denying that he is Jesus' disciple. The contrast may be part of the Evangelist's exhortation to Christians to remain faithful in their testimony to Jesus.

John's source seems to have contained an explanation of how Peter got into the house; he was with a disciple who was known to the high priest. Ingenious attempts have been made to explain such an unlikely acquaintanceship, but attempts to identify the disciple with the beloved disciple are unsatisfactory because the Evangelist always identifies the beloved disciple. The whole incident is the type that is added to a story to explain a difficulty; however, the anonymous disciple has not been worked into the rest of the narrative. The question put to Peter and his denial, more direct than in the synoptics, probably reflect later interrogations of Christians. Peter is asked if he is a disciple of Jesus, and he denies it.

Annas Interrogates Jesus

Annas asks Jesus about his disciples and his teaching. These questions may have both religious and political overtones, for both considerations have been part of the Jews' proceedings against Jesus: They consider him a blasphemer and false prophet, and are worried about the political consequences of his following. The question about Jesus' disciples may have been aimed at determining if they would start an uprising (as feared in 11:48). Of course, the reader knows that Jesus' followers had been forbidden to take such action (v. 11). Further irony is added by the fact that we have just seen one of Jesus' disciples deny that he is a disciple—and he was the one who was thinking of fighting.

Throughout the trial narrative the Evangelist arranges scenes which alternate between Jesus' being interrogated inside and others being questioned outside. He can thus contrast Jesus' testimony to himself with what others say about him.

The religious accusation against Jesus could also be included in the question about the disciples. The false prophet deserved death because he led others astray by not speaking what is from God. Jesus has countered that charge throughout the narrative by insisting that his message is from God. He refers to the earlier controversy stories (cf. 7:26ff., 8:20, 26, 10:24–26).

Jesus' demand that they ask witnesses about his teaching may be ironic. First, the witnesses Jesus has called in earlier controversies (e.g., 5:31ff., 8:13ff.) are not people. Second, Nicodemus had earlier chastised the Jews for trying Jesus without having heard from him, himself (7:51). This verse may also look forward to the later disciples, who will have to testify to what they have seen and heard from Jesus (15:27; cf. 1 Jn 1:1–3).

All versions report that Jesus was abused during his interrogation, but John's version is the least severe. In the synoptics, Jesus remains silent during the abuse, which is a challenge to prophesy. Brown (2:836) points out that the silence of Jesus fits the picture of the servant as one who remains silent before his tormentors in Is 53:3–7. In John,

Jesus answers by asserting his innocence. He answers all questions in the Johannine trial narrative except those about his origins (19:9). Just as the previous episode ended with a question in which Jesus announced his intention to suffer, this one ends with his insisting that he is innocent of all the charges against him.

Peter's Denial Concluded

This section of the gospel ends with denials by Peter. Perhaps the Evangelist has omitted the indication of Peter's reaction in other accounts because he has already told us enough to show that Jesus' prophecy was fulfilled (13:38).

John 18:28-40 *Jesus before Pilate*

The trial is divided into scenes that alternate between the outside and the inside of the praetorium. The Evangelist has focused the entire narrative on the question of Jesus' kingship. The formal Roman charge, according to the titulus on the cross, was that Jesus was a political revolutionary, "king of the Jews." To show the true nature of Jesus' kingship, the Evangelist has made changes in the traditional presentation; he has added dialogue between Pilate and the parties involved, and abbreviated some longer episodes.

John 18:28-32 *Jews Bring Jesus to Pilate*

The location of the praetorium is still debated; it could have been a palace (built by Herod) on the western hill or the fortress Antonia, which overlooked the temple area. Nor has it been possible to find a satisfactory explanation for the claim that the Jewish leaders would not go in lest they be defiled (v. 28). Perhaps this motif is a literary device to keep them outside and to contrast their concern to eat the Passover lamb with their determination to have the true paschal lamb, Jesus, killed.

A Roman official would normally begin the day before dawn. In a trial *extra-ordinem,* such as this one, the pro-curator could set his own rules, but a formal charge had to be brought against the defendant. Pilate begins by asking for the required charge, but the Jews fail to bring one. Their failure highlights the Evangelist's contention that they have no case against Jesus. Pilate will eventually produce the charge "king of the Jews," and the Jews will finally admit that their charge, blasphemy, is religious and does not belong in a Roman court. Pilate's repeated demand that the Jews handle the case themselves points out that they are the offended party; Jesus has done nothing wrong under Roman law. Legal historians agree that the claim that they could not put Jesus to death (v. 31) is probably correct. The Evangelist explains the fact that Jesus was crucified for a religious charge, which carried the penalty of stoning, by referring to the necessity for his death to take the form of "lifting up" (cf. 12:32f.).

John 18:33–38a *Jesus' Kingship*

Pilate begins this typically Johannine dialogue by trying to specify a charge against Jesus. Although Pilate is con-cerned with the literal, political charge, Jesus speaks about his heavenly mission. Pilate insists that the Jews are re-sponsible. John is more careful than the other evangelists not to implicate the whole Jewish people in Jesus' death.

The chief priests and Pharisees are presented as the ones opposed to Jesus (cf. 35b).

Jesus immediately explains that his kingship is not political. No one is fighting to free him (the reader knows that he has forbidden such action). Pilate does not understand, but he picks up the word "king" and asks for more information. Jesus answers with a solemn proclamation, which links true understanding of his kingship to the fulfillment of his mission. The opening remark to Pilate, "You say that I am a king," may indicate that although the Evangelist thinks Jesus can rightly be called "king of Israel" (1:49, 12:13), though he does not accept the title as used by Pilate. It can be properly understood only by someone who has accepted Jesus as the one sent from God.

The reader recognizes Jesus' statement in verses 36-37 as a summary of his mission, much like the summary in 3:31-36, in which the person who "accepts" Jesus is said to attest that God is true. Debate over the truth revealed by Jesus played a major role in the controversy stories (e.g., 8:40-47). Pilate's question, "What is truth?" shows that he is not one of those who "hears" Jesus' voice. He cannot understand what is being said to him and will not— as the rest of the narrative makes clear—respond to the truth.

John 18:38b-40 *The Barabbas Incident*

The four versions of the Barabbas incident (see chart in Brown, 2:870) are sufficiently similar to suggest a common, early tradition behind them. There is no extrabiblical evidence for a Passover amnesty. On the other hand, such a story would seem to require some historical basis—perhaps a unique event that occurred at the time of Jesus' death (Brown 2:870f.). John has abbreviated the incident and switched the initiative from the crowd to Pilate (p. Mk 15:8). These changes fit the drama of the trial, in which, ironically, the Jews are forced into rejecting their true salvation: Jesus as Passover lamb, shepherd, king of Israel, and Son of God—in favor of subjection to Rome. Although the word that is used for Barabbas, *lestes,* often meant a zealot or religio-political revolutionary, John seems to use the term in the more general sense, "robber." (His source may have capitalized on the political charge: Jesus died as a so-called zealot while the real zealot went free.) John used *lestes* as "robber" in the parable about the good shepherd (10:1, 8), which is probably the contrast he sees here.

The opening episodes of the trial have made the relationships between the parties clear. The Jewish leaders have no real case against Jesus but are determined to have him killed, even at the price of losing their hopes for salvation. Pilate will go along with them because he cannot "hear" Jesus' voice; but, in so doing, he will expose the real nature of what the Jews are doing. Jesus is innocent of all charges. The only manifestation of his kingship in this world is the group of believers who have accepted his revelation, and they will not fight for his release because his kingship is not a socio-political designation. It is one of many ways to express the fact that Jesus is the true Revealer and Savior of Israel.

These stories may also serve as examples to persecuted Christians of how they must deal with charges brought against Jesus and themselves.

19. Condemnation and Death of Jesus

Jesus emerged from the interrogations of the previous chapter as the only one who stands for the truth under questioning. He insists on his innocence and the divine sanction of his mission. Peter, on the other hand, denied being a disciple. The Jewish leaders will lay aside their hopes for salvation to have Jesus condemned. Pilate shows himself unable to respond to the truth, even though he perceives that Jesus is innocent under Roman law. All these forces come together in the condemnation and death of Jesus. Peter will be replaced by the positive image of discipleship (elsewhere always associated with him): the beloved disciple.

John 19:1–3 *Crowning with Thorns*

The first scene between Jesus and Pilate established that Jesus is king. John has moved the mockery and beating of Jesus from its traditional—and legal—setting: after the sentencing to the center of the trial. He also seems to have abbreviated the description of the mockery so that the focus of the scene is on Jesus, invested as king and paid homage as such. Nothing could make the claim that Jesus' kingship is not of this world clearer than this scene. At the same time, the soldiers do not remove the kingly garments (contrast Mk 15:20); so Jesus goes through the rest of the trial clad as king.

219

John 19:4-7 *Behold the Man*

Some exegetes think this scene reflects kingship rituals in which the new king, clad in his robes, was led out before his subjects and his throne name announced. If so, the entire incident is highly ironic.

Pilate first announces that he considers Jesus innocent (v. 4). Then he presents Jesus to the crowd. His words, "Behold the man," have occasioned many interpretations. Are they to elicit pity? Are they sarcastic? Or was "man" a messianic title in Hellenistic Judaism? Although the latter would fit the kingship motif best, the evidence for such a title is weak. Pity does not fit the characterization of Pilate in this gospel; therefore, we understand the remark as sarcastic. It reflects Pilate's general contempt for the Jews (cp. 18:34b) and directs attention to Jesus as he has been attired—as their king.

Note that only the chief priests and their police are involved in calling for Jesus' death. The people as a whole are not responsible.

Pilate's insistence that there is no Roman charge against Jesus finally forces the Jews to bring one. Thus John makes it clear that Jesus could not be charged under Roman law. The Jews are asking Pilate to carry out the sentence mandated for blasphemy in their law. But since Pilate cannot try someone under Jewish law, he will issue a Roman charge (19:15, 19), which the Jewish leaders do not wish to accept: Jesus is their king.

John 19:8-11 *Dialogue on Power*

As the trial winds to its conclusion, the Evangelist reminds us again that Jesus' death is not ultimately a victory for his opponents. The Jews had claimed that Jesus deserved death for blasphemously claiming equality with God; but we are not to think that Jesus' death proves them right. The dialogue is not a general discussion of the origin of political power or of the Roman *imperium* in particular; it refers specifically to Pilate's claim that he has the power to release or execute Jesus (v. 9). No one has power over Jesus (cf. 14:30f.); everything that happens to him happens according to the Father's will.

It is not clear why Pilate is said to be afraid in verse 8. Perhaps the Evangelist intends it as a response to "Son of God" in verse 7, much as the soldiers responded to the divine I AM (18:6). Schnackenburg (3:300) proposes that the fear motif plays into a subtle reversal which occurs in this scene. Pilate, the Roman procurator, is afraid; Jesus is not. Although Pilate is the judge, Jesus' answer to his statement about power not only asserts that Jesus is independent of human authorities (cf. 10:17f.) but represents Jesus' sentence against his opponents. Pilate is guilty; he did not respond to the truth. The Jewish authorities who handed Jesus over and have been clamoring for his death are even more guilty.

John 19:12–16a *No King but Caesar*

The final trial scene is a dialogue between Pilate and the Jews on kingship. Pilate forces the Jews to become supporters of the hated Roman empire. In later Roman times, "friend of Caesar" was an honorific title, based on special service to the emperor. The threat that Pilate might be accused of disloyalty was a real one in his day; the emperor was notoriously paranoid about treason, and many such charges were brought against leading citizens. To make the accusation that Pilate fosters enemies of the empire, however, the Jews must accept some form of claim to kingship by Jesus: "he makes himself king of the Jews."

Pilate brings Jesus outside again and seats himself on the judgment seat to pass sentence. His presentation of "their king" to the Jews leads, first, to the demand that Jesus be crucified and, second, to a renunciation of all kings but Caesar. Thus, ironically, the very desire to have Jesus executed, lest the Romans destroy the Jewish nation (11:48-50), leads the Jews to betray their long-held conviction that the only king is God. They have hailed Caesar as king. Further, they do so at the time when the Passover lamb—for the feast that celebrates their liberation from bondage—is being slaughtered in the temple.

The description of Jesus' being handed over is ambiguous. In the context, "them" would refer to the Jews, just as Pilate has consistently said that "they" should execute Jesus themselves, but the sentence of a Roman court had to be carries out by Roman soldiers.

John 19:16b-30 *Crucifixion of Jesus*

Many details in the synoptic crucifixion and burial accounts do not appear in John: Simon of Cyrene, the drugged potion, an indication of the time, incidents of mockery, darkness and other natural reactions at the death of Jesus, the centurion, women at the burial. Some may not have been in the Evangelist's sources; he may omit others to shift the focus of a story. Where we do not recognize a literary or theological pattern as characteristic of the Evangelist, we may assume that he is following a source. Unlike the trial scene, which had been thoroughly reworked into a series of episodes, this material consists of a skeleton of traditional material, which the Evangelist has changed only internally.

Titulus over the Cross

It is impossible to say whether John did not know a "way of the cross" or whether he omits it in order to stress Jesus' continued control over the situation. Jesus carries his own cross (v. 17). The Evangelist has focused on the dialogue between Pilate and the Jews over the titulus, the notice of the offense placed over the cross (vv. 20–22). All passion accounts agree that "king of the Jews" was the posted charge (v. 20). The dialogue continues the pattern that was set in the trial narrative: The Jews are reluctant to have the title, "king of the Jews," posted, but Pilate forces it upon them. The Jewish leaders take the charge as a statement which some might recognize as true, and do not wish to have it publicly proclaimed. The assertion that Golgotha was close enough to the city that many people could see the crucified has symbolic significance in John. John 12:32 predicted that when Jesus is "lifted up" he will draw all to him. Here, his universal kingship is exhibited in a multilingual inscription that anyone in Palestine could read. (The synoptics say nothing about the language of the inscription.)

Dividing Jesus' Garments

This scene is longer than in the synoptics. Mark 15:24 and Lk 23:34 merely cite the OT text (Ps 22:19), while Mt 27:35 incorporates the quotation into a sentence describing what the soldiers do. The scene does not show any obvious characteristics of the Evangelist's reworking; so he probably derived it from his source. It shows that both parts of the quotation have been fulfilled: dividing the garments and casting dice for them.

Mother of Jesus and the Disciple at the Cross

No completely satisfactory explanation of the significance of this scene for the Evangelist has been given. The awkward transition in 24c, the inclusion of the mother of Jesus and the beloved disciple, and Jesus' concern for his disciples (cf. 18:8) are all characteristic of the Evangelist. He may have found a reference to the women's viewing the crucifixion from a distance, similar to Lk 23:49, in his source and turned that reference into a scene to form a pair with that of the soldiers. In the synoptic accounts, attempts to give Jesus drugged wine might suggest that Jesus was dazed or losing consciousness at the end, but not here. Jesus is completely conscious of everything that happens, and can even direct the future of his followers.

Verse 28 suggests that the Evangelist sees this as the concluding scene in Jesus' ministry. The mother of Jesus has not appeared since the "opening" scene at Cana, where she was told that Jesus' hour had not yet come. Then Jesus was said to have manifested his glory and led his disciples to believe in him (2:12). Now it is the hour of his glorification, and she is again present with the beloved disciple.

Her presence may also remind the reader of Ps 22:9-10, where the protection of God is linked with the care that the sufferer received from his mother:

Yet Thou art he who took me from the womb;
Thou didst keep me safe upon my mother's breasts.
Upon Thee was I cast from my birth,
    and since my mother bore me Thous hast been my God.
    [RSV]

In the synoptics, the immediately preceding verses underlie the mockery of the crucified (cf. Mk 15:29 parr.), a scene John does not recount. The next verse pleads for God to help the sufferer who has been deserted: "Be not far from me, for trouble is near and there is no one to help." John 16:32 spoke of Jesus as being left alone by all but the Father at the crucifixion—even though that is not the case in this scene. If our suggestion that Ps 22 underlies this scene is correct, the presence of Jesus' mother provides a powerful image of divine presence and protection in the midst of the brutality and hostility of the crucifixion, a brutality that is evoked in the Psalm text as well. Further, the presence of the beloved disciple, who is often symbolic of the Christian, assures the reader that the same loving protection continues with the community. Compare 17:26, where the Father's love for Jesus is said to be with the disciples.

If the woman also represents the birth pangs by which Zion brings forth her children in the new age (Is 49:20ff.) and the new Eve (Gn 4:1), the episode implies that those children (= the Christians) have been born. Jesus' messianic mission is finished.

John 19:28-30 *Jesus Dies*

Jesus continues deliberately to fulfill his mission. John does not specify which OT passage Jesus' thirst fulfills. Psalm 22:15—which was quoted in the previous two scenes—mentions the thirst of the sufferer but not the sour wine. Psalm 69:21 says that the enemies of the sufferer gave him sour wine to drink. Both psalms occur throughout early Christian apologetic, and the Evangelist may have had a combination of the two in mind. A hyssop could not have supported the weight of a sponge; so perhaps the verse is an allusion to the use of a hyssop in sprinkling the blood of the Passover lamb

(Ex 12:22). Jesus announces that he has carried out the work of the Father (cp. 14:31, 17:4). He does not die passively, but hands his life over the the Father.

John 19:31–37 *Piercing Jesus' Side*

This incident is unique to John, so it is difficult to say what he may have derived from a source and what he may have added. On stylistic grounds, Schnackenburg (3:334f.) suggests that the phrase "for it was the great day of that Sabbath" (v. 31), and possible verse 37, were from the Evangelist, that verse 35 came from a later editor, and that the rest is from a source. The episode also provides a contrast with the following burial scene.

The skeleton of a crucified man that was found in a Jerusalem cemetery shows that the legs had been broken at the time of death, while the body was still on the cross. The actions attributed to the soldiers here (vv. 32f.) agree with what seems to have been the practice.

The blood and water, said to have flowed from the side of Jesus, could reflect the ancient medical view that a person's body fluids are blood and water. This view influenced an earlier Jewish martyrdom story about seven brothers who were tortured to death for refusing to renounce Judaism. One brother is broken on a wheel and roasted by live coals, "and the whole wheel is besmeared with his blood and the heaped coals were quenched by the humours of his body, dripping down [on them]" (IV Macc 9:20). Throughout these tortures the young man speaks out, encouraging his brothers to follow his example, and at the end he "yielded up his spirit." Thus it may be that the language about Jesus' death in John's source was influenced by Jewish martyrological traditions.

But the Evangelist probably sees deeper significance in the blood and water. Sacrificial ritual requires that the blood of the victim flow freely, so that is could be sprinkled. John 7:38f. associates rivers of living water, to come from the heart of Jesus, with the Spirit that is to be given when Jesus is glorified. The symbolism would suggest that Jesus' death/exaltation has accomplished that salvation.

Verse 35 seems to have been added by a later disciple, since it closely resembles the remark about the beloved disciple in 21:24 (cp. 1 Jn 5:6f.). This verse shows that the Johannine community read the passage in a symbolic sense; otherwise, it would not have been necessary to back up the scene with an appeal to eyewitness testimony.

Verse 35 separates the incident from the OT quotations it is said to fulfill, but it is not clear which OT passage is meant by the reference to breaking his bones. Psalm 22:14 describes broken bones as part of the sufferer's fate, as does the martyrological tradition. Psalm 34:20 says that although many afflictions overwhelm the righteous, the Lord "keeps all his bones; not one of them shall be broken." This tradition of the suffering righteous was probably the one referred to in the source. John also associates Jesus' death with the Passover lamb; so he may see the quotation as a reference to the rule that none of the lamb's bones are to be broken (Ex 12:46, Nm 9:12).

The piercing is explained by an allusion to Zec 12:10. Psalm 22:16 also refers to piercing the victim but lacks the "they will see" of the Zechariah passage, which occurs elsewhere in passion apologetic. This passage was used to suggest that those who has crucified Jesus would mourn when they saw him return as judge (Rv 1:7). This image may also underlie the Johannine passion predictions, which speak of people looking upon or seeing the Son of Man raised up (3:14f., 8:29, 12:32) and the stress on the many who saw

Jesus crucified (19:20). Although the Zechariah quote is usually a judgment oracle, John may intend his reader to think of the earlier prophecies of the crucifixion. Jesus' enemies are already condemned by their rejection of him. The believers, on the other hand, look upon the crucified and are saved.

The allusions to OT texts throughout the crucifixion narrative and the reminders of what he has said before about the crucifixion give the Evangelist's readers a dramatic assessment of Jesus' mission. He has concluded his mission by dying at the hands of godless and vicious men, like the suffering righteous in the OT. Like the righteous, he does so out of love for God and under God's constant care and protection. Further, he shows that same care and concern for his disciples. In so dying, Jesus has provided true salvation.

John 19:38-42 *Burial of Jesus*

John's source probably had Joseph of Arimathea ask for the body, wrap it, and put it in a new tomb before the Sabbath (cp. Mk 15:42-47)—that much is common to all versions. It may have included an unnamed person with the spices (cf. Lk 23:56, an unnamed woman). The Evangelist has explained that Joseph was a secret disciple "for fear of the Jews" (cp. 9:22); he identified Joseph's associate as Nicodemus, and inserted a remark about Jewish burial custom (v. 40b). No convincing hypothesis has been offered to link this scene to the major themes of Johannine theology. The Evangelist's parenthetical remark about burial customs suggests that he found the incident unusual and attributed it to Jewish custom.

The burial scene concludes the passion narrative. It makes it clear that Jesus was really dead. He was not in a coma, to be revived by disciples, who spirited away the body—as ancient and modern opponents of Christianity have sometimes suggested. Nor—a point stressed in the next chapter, where Jesus is said not to have ascended yet (20:17)—did he ascend directly into heaven, like a divine emanation, and leave the body behind like a temporary costume. Despite the divinity of Jesus and his closeness to the Father, which have been stressed throughout the narrative, the Evangelist would not have us suppose that his death and burial were somehow unreal. The martyrological tradition shows that consciousness and encouragement to others could be expected of the righteous person, who faces death out of love for God. These features of the Johannine account demonstrate that what Jesus does is in accord with the will of God; he is not a criminal or sinner. Nor does his divinity "save him in the end." Jesus died and was buried.

20. Resurrection Appearances in Jerusalem

This chapter contains two sets of resurrection appearances. Two are at the tomb: first, Peter and the beloved disciple (vv. 1-10); then Mary Magdelene (vv. 1, 11-18). Then a pair occurs at meals: first, to the disciples (vv. 19-23); then to that group and Thomas (vv. 24-29). The Evangelist has created this pattern of paired stories, and the Thomas incident is entirely his composition. He has inserted references to faith in verses 8, 17, and 21-22, which are epitomized in that story, and has added the beloved disciple to the story of Peter's visit to the tomb. Verse 8 contrasts him with Thomas, since he believes—even though he has seen very little, even though he has only folded grave clothes. He thus represents ideal faith in the resurrection.

Source of the Empty-Tomb Stories

The empty-tomb stories show clear signs that the Evangelist derived them from a source. A variety of internal inconsistencies has resulted from the way in which he edited them into a whole. For example:

1. In verse 1 Mary is alone; her report to Peter says *"we do not know . . . "*

2. She reports the body stolen (v. 2) but she has not looked in the tomb (v. 11).

3. Addition of the beloved disciple has led to duplications of what he and Peter see (cp. vv. 4 and 6, 8 and 9). Further, his faith (v. 8) plays no role in the rest of the narrative.

4. When Mary enters the tomb she finds angels (v. 12), whereas Peter has not seen angels but burial clothes.

5. Mary had left the garden to report to Peter and was never said to return. Her conversation with the angels plays no part in the action. She is said to turn toward Jesus twice.

These inconsistencies, as well as comparison with other resurrection appearances, suggest that the Evangelist had at least two accounts of the events at the tomb from which he formulated his narrative. There must have been a description of the finding of the empty tomb by several women, who are commissioned to go and tell the disciples that Jesus is risen (cp. Mk 16:1-8 parr.). The Evangelist typically reduces group scenes to focus on a single individual, and he probably singled out Mary Magdelene because of her importance in the tradition. The second source was an account in which several disciples come to the tomb to check the women's report. Luke 24:12 and 24 allude to such a tradition. Once again the author has focused on key individuals, Peter and the beloved disciple.

All the stories are told in such a way as to indicate that true faith in the risen Jesus does not depend upon one's ability to see, hear, or touch him but on the conviction that the one sent by the Father has returned to him in glory. This belief is as accessible to later believers as to the first disciples. Thus verses 28b-29 sum up the message of the chapter.

John 20:1-10 *The Empty Tomb*

The introduction to the women's visit to the tomb now serves as the introduction to both stories. Mary Magdelene becomes the only one to visit the tomb, and she reports to Peter. The "we do not know" of her report (v. 2) shows that the original had more than one woman visit the tomb—as do the other versions. Her concern that someone may have taken the body suggests that the story of the disciples' visit may have been intended to disprove the accusation that the disciples had stolen the body (cp. Mt 28:13-15, which treats that accusation in a different fashion). Perhaps the unusual disposition of the burial clothes was intended to be evidence that the tomb had not been robbed. The original story would have ended with the disciples' leaving in perplexity (so v. 9). Compare Lk 24:13-27, where the risen Jesus explains to the disciples, who are perplexed by everything that has happened, including the empty tomb, that Scripture had predicted the Messiah would suffer and so enter into his glory. John has consistently presented the crucifixion as Jesus' entry into glory.

To introduce the beloved disciple into the story, the Evangelist has "doubled" the description of the arrival at the tomb. Perhaps the beloved disciple arrives first as a symbol of his examplary faith and closeness to Jesus. Then, by having him enter the tomb last, the Evangelist makes his faith the culminating statement about the empty-tomb story (v. 8). Contrary to verse 9 and the other versions, which make it clear that the empty tomb was not proof to the disciples that Jesus had been raised, the beloved disciple believes solely on the basis of the burial clothes—no angel, no appearance of Christ, is necessary for him. His faith is the climax of the story. It is also the faith which the Evangelist knows is demanded of his readers, who will not have had the experiences of the first disciples.

For John, then, faith in the resurrection is, from the beginning, belief in Jesus. It is not something for which proofs can be offered. Perhaps he retains verse 9, after the statement about the beloved disciple's faith, because he knows that although the resurrection had been predicted (2:22), the disciples did not yet have something which later believers have: the understanding that Jesus' death and resurrection fulfill Scripture.

John 20:11-18   *Jesus Appears to Mary Magdelene*

Unless it originally came before Peter's visit to the tomb, this story derives from another source than the previous one. Mary is never said to return to the tomb; she sees angels, not burial wrappings. This story is similar to Mt 28:1-10, where Mary Magdelene and another Mary come to the tomb; find an angel, who tells them that Jesus is risen and sends them to the disciples; meet the risen Jesus on the way back; worship him; and are sent to deliver to the disciples the same message the angel had given them. In Matthew, the angel knows what they are seeking. Here, dialogue has been introduced. The angel asks Mary why she mourns (Lk 24:5), and she repeats the message she had given to Peter. Rather than have a double commissioning, as in Matthew, John has her turn around and repeat the dialogue with Jesus, who she thinks is a gardener.

Many of the resurrection stories contain the motif of non-recognition. The risen Jesus must identify himself through a symbolic act or greeting, as in Mt 28:9a. Since Jews believed that the resurrected body would be transformed and glorified, such non-recognition might well be expected. The risen Jesus is not just a corpse revivified, as in some of the healings he has performed; he cannot be understood to have emerged from a deathlike coma. Many of the symbolic actions he performs have the additional function of pointing out that there is a real continuity between the earthly and the risen Jesus. The disciples do not see some ghost or apparition. The recognition scene in this story, where Jesus calls Mary and she clings to him, was probably part of the source, where the clinging would have been an act of worship—

perhaps prostrating herself at Jesus' feet, as in Mt 29:9.

The Evangelist probably understands the symbolism of Mary's being called by name in relation to his earlier statement that Jesus' sheep recognize his voice. Her recognition of him shows that she is truly a disciple. But John has switched the form of her response from worship to clinging, which is not an acceptable response to the risen Lord. Jesus' words to Mary are typically Johannine; they fulfill the prediction in 6:62: "What if you should see the Son of Man ascending to where he was before?" Throughout the last discourses, Jesus stressed the fact that his real return would not be seen by the world (cf. 14:18f., 16:22). It would not be a cosmic, apocalyptic vision of the Son of Man, as the tradition behind 6:62 probably suggested.

In chapter 14, the return is accomplished when the Father and Son dwell with the disciples, who must realize the necessity for Jesus to go to the Father (16:7). What Jesus says here, then, is that he has not yet gone to the Father. Therefore, the resurrection appearances are not the return that was promised in the discourses.

The Evangelist is not implying that there is some difference in the risen Jesus, prior to his ascension, that means Mary cannot touch him now, although Thomas will be challenged to do so later. Rather, he wishes to point out that Mary's clinging to the risen Lord denies the true significance of the event: Jesus returns to the Father and to the glory he had before the beginning of the world. (The expression in v. 17b may be derived from such OT passages as Lv 26:12 or Ez 36:38.) Thus this story makes a point similar to that in the previous one: true faith in the risen Jesus recognizes his presence in heaven with God; it does not depend upon earthly visions. Note that Jesus' message to the disciples does not include any promise of a vision. Rather, his message is that he is returning to the Father, as he had said he would do.

John 20:19-23 *Appearance to the Disciples*

The Evangelist seems to have added the "fear of the Jews" motif and verse 21 to a story which originally associated forgiveness of sins within the community and a resurrection appearance to the disciples. The story in Lk 24:36-49 has many features in common with this one:

1. Jesus comes into the midst of the disciples (Lk 24:36, Jn 20:19).
2. Greeting: "Peace be to you" (Lk 24:36, Jn 20:19).
3. Shows his wounds (Lk 24:39, Jn 20:20).
4. Says to rejoice (Lk 24:41, Jn 20:20).
5. In Lk 24:47-49 they are told to preace forgiveness of sins and are promised the Spirit; in Jn 20:22f. they are actually given the spirit and the power to forgive sins.

The Lucan story is longer and more elaborate than the Johannine, but the parallels show that a similar tradition was known to both. The expression for "binding" and forgiving sins is similar to the power over sins granted the community in Mt 16:19//18:19. The association of that power with the gift of the Spirit suggests that the Evangelist is not thinking of developments in penitential discipline but of the forgiveness of sins brought by the Spirit in baptism. The "binding" of sin may have been understood as part of the disciples' mission to the world. Insofar as people reject Jesus and their preaching, they would be condemned.

When the Evangelist added verse 21 to the story, he brought it into line with the commissioning language of the farewell discourses (cp. 17:17-19). Therefore, most interpreters today see the gift of the Spirit as a promise to the whole community. The Evangelist does not associate it with a particular office or subgroup.

John 20:24–29 *Appearance to Thomas*

This story is entirely made up of Johannine themes. The previous stories had been arranged to reflect the Evangelist's view that true resurrection faith is in Jesus' return to the Father; it does not depend upon physical appearances. In the previous story, the commissioning of the disciples by the risen Jesus did not add anything to what the earthly Jesus had done at the Last Supper. They were sent, as he had been. Thus the mission of the Church is not founded upon the appearances of the risen Jesus but upon his commission prior to his death.

Since the first chapter, discipleship stories have followed a set pattern: A person hears about Jesus from someone else; then comes to Jesus and, after dialogue with him, confesses his faith. This story follows that pattern. Verses 24–25 have the disciples tell Thomas that they have seen the Lord. ("To see the Lord" was the standard confession of resurrection faith [cf. v. 18].) Instead of responding with belief, Thomas demands even more proof than the disciples had been given. Jesus returns when Thomas is present and takes up his challenge. Just as the Evangelist shows little interest in the outcome of miracle stories, so here: We are not told whether Thomas touched Jesus or not. We are told only about his confession that Jesus is Lord and God. This confession that Jesus is Lord and God. This confession is the high point of all the others in the gospel (e.g., 1:49, 4:42, 6:69, 9:37f., 11:27, 16:30): Jesus is God.

The macarism in verse 29 draws the moral of the story for all later believers, but the blessing is not designed to make a dichotomy between those who saw Jesus and later believers, who cannot. All must believe the same thing: Jesus is God, the one sent by the Father to reveal him and save the world, and he is now exalted in heaven with the

Father. The farewell discourses and the resurrection stories alike have made it clear that true faith in the risen Jesus and his eternal presence is the same for all believers.

John 20:30-31 *Conclusion*

These verses are the formal conclusion of the gospel (cp 21:24f; 1 Jn 5:13f). Since "sign" usually refers to the miracles of Jesus understood as manifestations of his glory, many interpreters think that John took the verses from the source he used for the miracles. They show a more positive assessment of the relationship between signs and belief than the rest of the gospel does. Jn 12:37, for example, is a negative echo of this conclusion: "But although he had done such signs before them, they did not believe in him." The evangelist does not think that miracles automatically engender faith. He can take over the conclusion of a work which speaks positively of signs because he is addressing later believers, who have believed without seeing. They know that Jesus is Lord and God. For them, a proper understanding of his testimony will bolster their faith in Jesus as messiah and Son of God in the face of opposition and hostility. The final connection between belief and having life is typically Johannine (cf. 3:15f, 36). By adding that motif to the conclusion, the evangelist sets his whole work within the context of the saving and life-giving testimony to Jesus, which the disciples are now commissioned to give.

21. Resurrection Appearance in Galilee

After 20:30f., one would not expect an additional chapter; nor does the story in this chapter presuppose earlier appearances. The disciples seem to have returned to their homes and former occupations; they do not recognize the risen Lord. It belongs to the tradition that Jesus appeared in Galilee (Mk and Mt) rather than in Jerusalem (Lk and Jn 20). As it stands, the chapter picks up themes from earlier chapters: shepherd/sheep, Peter/beloved disciple, testimony; and verse 13 reflects 6:11. Therefore, most exegetes suppose that this chapter, like chapters 15–17, was added to the gospel after the death of the Evangelist by one of his disciples—who is responsible for the explanation of the death of the beloved disciple in verses 23–24.

Traditions behind the Chapter

This chapter contains traditions which had been circulating in the Johannine community. Verses 1–11 are based on a story about an appearance to the disciples at the sea and a miraculous catch of fish. Verses 12–13 show that the miraculous-catch story had been combined with another about Jesus' appearance at a meal. The second half of the chapter relates the fate of the two heroes of the community, Peter (vv. 15–19) and the beloved disciple (vv. 20–23). Peter is the principal actor in all the episodes. Thus, in its present form, the chapter focuses on Peter's role and the consequences of the resurrection for the ongoing life of the community. By bringing the story through the death of the two key figures in the founding of the community, the author of this chapter shows that the commission Jesus gave the disciples was indeed carried out.

John 21:1-4 *Jesus Appears by the Sea*

This story has parallels in two synoptic stories, both associated with Peter. In Mt 14:28-33 Peter asks to walk on water, and has to be rescued. The story about Jesus' walking on water after the feeding of the 5,000 occurs in all four gospels. Some exegetes think Matthew has combined a post-resurrection story about Jesus and Peter with the miracle. Luke 5:1-11 associates the call of Peter with a miraculous catch of fish. There, too, the disciples have been fishing all night, are instructed to lower their nets, and catch so many fish that the nets are about to break. That story concludes with the commissioning of Peter and the others to become "fishers of men." Some think that this story too was originally a post-resurrection appearance (see Brown 2:1087-92). If so, the Johannine version of the miraculous catch—without the additions (vv. 9, 12, 13)—may represent an early form of the story.

Peter's decision to go fishing (v. 3) suggests that the disciples had returned to their occupations, and thus that the story is independent of those in chapter 20. No further commission to the disciples is needed after chapter 20. Verses 1-2 tie this story to the gospel. The motif of non-recognition is typical of resurrection stories. Jesus calls the disciples "little children," a designation that 1 John shows was typical of the Johannine community (1 Jn 2:13, 18, 3:7). The recognition of Jesus does not occur until after the fish are caught. The author has introduced the beloved disciple as the one to recognize the Lord, just as he had understood the significance of the empty tomb (20:8). This addition prepares the way for the second half of the chapter, which focuses on the beloved disciple and Peter.

John does not provide any clues as to how the catch of fish was understood. However, if the story is a variant of that in Lk 5, we may assume that the same interpretation applies to the catch of fish here: the large catch represents the success of the mission. Although the disciples are not commissioned here as "fishers of men," the story suggests such a commissioning by having Jesus request that some of the fish be brought to him (note that the same thing happens in the discipleship stories: people are brought to Jesus). Many exegetes suggest that the number of fish alludes to the universality of the mission; it will include all people: Jews, Samaritans, Gentiles. Perhaps the Johannine community saw the unbroken net as a reference to the theme of unity, so prominent in the farewell discourses. But the emphasis here would seem to fall more on internal unity—as it does in 1 John—than on external challenges as in the gospel.

John 20:9, 12-13 *Jesus Reveals Himself in a Meal*

A story about Jesus' self-revelation in a meal has been joined to that about the catch of fish. Verse 12 shows that the story originally had its own recognition scene, probably in the giving of bread (Lk 24:30-31, 35). The conclusion to verse 12, "knowing that it was the Lord," would have been added when the two stories were combined. Combination of two separate stories also accounts for the confusion between Jesus' request for fish (v. 10), part of the commissioning scene in the earlier story, and the fish Jesus had on the fire (vv. 9, 11).

Verse 13 makes the eucharistic symbolism of the meal

clear: Jesus takes bread and fish and distributes it to the disciples, as he had distributed the loaves and fishes in 6:11. Johannine tradition has given the fish and meal stories new significance by combining them. Although the combination is awkward, because the fish are future believers in the first story and part of the eucharistic meal in the second, the point is clear: All are called to the presence of Jesus, manifest in the eucharistic meal. The author emphasizes that point by putting the request for fish (v. 10) and Peter's emptying of the net (v. 11) between verses 9 and 12, which describe the meal.

We have seen that the Johannine resurrection tradition consistently emphasizes modes of presence and recognition that do not depend upon the miraculous appearance of Jesus. Both recognition scenes are clearly divorced from the literal fact of the resurrection. The beloved disciple first recognizes the Lord through the size of the catch (v. 7); the disciples come to the meal already knowing that it is the Lord.

Both modes of recognition are open to believers in any time or place; all can recognize Jesus' presence in the mission of the Church and in the Eucharist. The presence of the risen Lord is a permanent reality within the Christian community, not a historical event that has faded into the past. Therefore, belief in the resurrection is the same for us as for the disciples. All believers are called to the mission, to be "sent," and to the sacrament.

John 21:15-17 *Peter Is Commissioned*

This section preserves another tradition about Peter's commissioning. Like the previous one, it alludes to the missionary expansion of the Church. First, Peter's denial of

Jesus—in John, a denial that he was a disciple (cf. 18:17)—
is rectified by his threefold profession of love for Jesus. Although John is the only gospel in which Peter is formally
given a second chance, Lk 22:32 may reflect such a tradition. There, Jesus predicts that Peter will turn and strengthen
his brothers. Also, in the synoptic tradition, Peter weeps after
the denial. In Lk 22:61, Jesus looks at Peter and reminds
Peter of his words. The Johannine tradition may have associated Peter's repentance with his vision of the risen Lord.

Both Lk 22:32 and this passage associate Peter's repentance
with a specific mission: "strengthen your brothers" (Lk);
"feed my sheep" (Jn). This commission probably refers to
Peter's pre-eminence as a missionary (e.g., Ac 1 to 11; 1
Cor 1:12ff.). Similarly, in the previous story Peter was the
one to bring in the net. The sheep Peter is sent to feed are
probably the "other sheep" of Jn 10:16—they must be called
by the apostolic mission. Though some have seen the contrast
between Peter and the beloved disciple as an indication that
the Johannine community opposed the growing authority of
the Petrine tradition, this passage shows that it was well
aware of the important role Peter played in the growth and
establishment of the Church. All the gospels attribute his
significance to a commission received from Jesus, but all
are careful to point out that Peter was not always the ideal
disciple. He did not always understand what Jesus said to
him or act as one might expect a disciple to. This side of
the Peter story may have encouraged later Christians, who
were well aware of their own limitations and failures. At
the same time, the gospel places the beloved disciple alongside Peter. He shows how the ideal disciple would act and
thus provides a model for which the Christian should strive.
Peter shows that although the Christian may fail to testify
to Jesus at some point, he or she is not rejected. One can

still repent, as Peter has done, and take up the mission of witnessing to Jesus anew.

John 21:18-19 *Death of Peter*

Verse 18 preserves an independent saying in which Jesus predicts Peter's future. The saying does not clearly predict his death; it could even refer to general sufferings entailed by the apostolic mission (Jn 15:18ff.; cp. 2 Cor 11:23-33). The author's comment in verse 19 (cp. 12:33) shows that, at least after Peter's death, this saying was understood as a prediction of his martyrdom. The final command, "follow me," takes on a double meaning. It is the standard expression for becoming a disciple (cf. 1:37, 43, 10:27, 12:26). It can also refer to Jesus' prediction that Peter will follow him in death (13:36). Thus this verse shows that Peter, too, brought his mission to its proper fulfillment. Like Jesus, his death "glorified God" (cf. 7:39, 12:23, 17:45).

John 21:20-23 *The Beloved Disciple*

Although Peter was revered as a missionary by the Church at large, the Johannine community looked back to another disciple, the beloved disciple, as its founder. An account of the origins of the community would not be complete without reference to this revered figure; so the disciple-author of this chapter has Peter ask about that disciple. Peter's question does not imply a rivalry between the two but brings the beloved disciple under the same commissioning as that attributed to Peter.

Verse 22 seems to be an independent saying, similar to the one about Peter in verse 18. Similar sayings in the synoptic tradition (e.g., Mk 9:1ff., Mt 10:23, 16:28) promise that some of those listening to Jesus will not die before the second coming. The Johannine community may have used such a saying about the beloved disciple to explain why he did not suffer a martyr's death, like Peter and many of the other early apostles. The early Christians so honored those who had followed Jesus to the point of death that they sometimes had to be restrained from seeking the glory of martydom. This exchange between Jesus and Peter teaches that each person must accept the mode of following that Jesus designated for him or her, and not worry about whether another person's path is more glorious. The next verse shows that the beloved disciple had died before this chapter was written; so the author must correct those who had understood Jesus' saying as a prediction that the beloved disciple would not die.

John 21:24–25 *Conclusion*

This conclusion is modeled on Jn 20:30. It points out that the Johannine community ("we know") derived its tradition from the beloved disciple. John 19:35 made a similar appeal to his testimony about the crucifixion. Perhaps, since that disciple is paralleled with Peter, he was the founder of the community. The "these things" he is said to have written may not refer to the gospel. Internal references to the exclusion of Christians from the synagogue lead us to date the gospel after A.D. 90, but we have seen that the gospel depends upon earlier tradition. Therefore, most modern exegetes (e.g., Brown, 2:1128–30; Schnackenburg, 3:446) hold that these words refer to the oral teaching and preaching of the disciple as it was preserved in the community. (The Essenes at Qumran had a similar practice of referring to their founder and the source of their tradition by a pseudonym.)

Modeled on 20:31, verse 25 reiterates the theme that the author knows other traditions that are not contained in the gospel. Hyperbolic statements about the extent of other traditions may have been literary commonplaces (cp. Eccl 12:9–12).

In a sense, the final chapter has brought us through another stage in the ministry of Jesus: its continuation by the first generation of apostles. We saw that the farewell discourses commissioned Jesus' disciples to take his mission to the world. The marvelous catch of fish implies a similar commission. At the same time, the extent of the catch suggests that their mission has had great results. The chapter is capped by the author's reflection on the death of the two great heroes of that generation, Peter and the beloved disciple. Both fulfilled the mission Jesus had set for them and thus had glorified God. Subsequent generations of those who have not seen and yet believe (20:29b) have the same resurrection faith. Jesus is present in the continuing mission of the Church and in her eucharistic celebration. Subsequent disciples who share that presence must follow the example of these disciples in bearing true witness to the revelation of God in Jesus Christ (cp. 1 Jn 1:1–5).

Bibliography and Suggestions
for
Further Reading

"Introduction"

Kysar, R., *The Fourth Evangelist and His Gospel.* Minneapolis: Augsburg, 1975. A detailed survey of Johannine scholarship.

MacRae, G., *Faith in the Word: The Fourth Gospel.* Chicago: Franciscan Herald Press, 1973. An excellent introductory essay.

Perkins, P., *Gospel of St. John.* Chicago: Franciscan Herald Press, 1975. A short commentary for devotional reading.

"Commentary"

Barrett, C. K., *The Gospel according to St. John.* London: SPCK, 1967. Requires some knowledge of Greek.

Brown, R., *The Gospel according to John, I-XII (AncBi 29), XIII-XXI (AncBi 29A).* New York: Doubleday, 1966/70. A massive achievement by one of the leading Johannine scholars of the day. Full bibliographies on every passage. (Abbreviated Brown 1, Brown 2.)

Lindars, B., *The Gospel of John.* London: Oliphants, 1972. For the nonspecialist; based on the RSV.

Schnackenburg, R., *The Gospel according to St. John. Vol. I: Chs. 1-4.* New York: Herder, 1968. English translation of *Das Johannesevangelium. Kap. 1-4. (HTKNT IV, 1).* Freiburg: Herder, 1965. The remaining two volumes have not been translated (Vol. II: *Kap 5-12 (HTKNT IV, 2),* 1971; Vol. III: *Kap. 13-21 (HTKNT IV, 3),* 1975). A monumental work, which also concerns itself with the theology of the Evangelist. (Abbreviated Schnackenburg 1, Schnackenburg 2; Schnackenburg 3.)

Books

Barrett, C. K., *The Gospel of John and Judaism.* London: SPCK, 1975. Series of short lectures.

Cullmann, O., *The Johannine Circle.* Philadelphia: Westminster, 1976. An attempt to locate the historical context of the Johannine community.

Dodd, C. H., *Historical Tradition in the Fourth Gospel.* New York: Cambridge University Press, 1963. Detailed investigation of the tradition behind the gospel.

————. *The Interpretation of the Fourth Gospel.* New York: Cambridge University Press, 1953. An important study of the relationship between John and Jewish-Hellenistic mystical and philosophical traditions.

Forestell, J. T., *The Word of the Cross: Salvation as Revelation in the Fourth Gospel.* Rome: BIP, 1974. Important study of John's view of salvation.

Kaesemann, E., *The Testament of Jesus according to Jn 17.* Philadelphia: Fortress Press, 1968. A provocative work, which tries to argue that the Christology of John is docetic.

Martyn, J. L., *History and Theology in the Fourth Gospel.* New York: Harper & Row, 1968. Very readable discussion of the debate with Judaism as reflected in the gospel.

Meeks, W., *The Prophet-King: Moses Traditions and Johannine Christology.* Leiden: E. J. Brill, 1967. A thorough study of Jewish Moses traditions.

Schnackenburg, R., *Present and Future.* South Bend: University of Notre Dame Press, 1966. Has chapters on faith, salvation, and Christology in John: for the general reader.

Articles

Borgen, P., "God's Agent in the Fourth Gospel." *In Religious in Antiquity (In memory of E. R. Goodenough)*, Ed. J. Neusner. Leiden: E. J. Brill, 1968. Pp. 137-48.

Haenchen, E., "History and Interpretation in the Johannine Passion Narrative," *Interpretation* 24 (1970) 198-219.

MacRae, G., "The Ego-Proclamation in Gnostic Sources." In *The Trial of Jesus, Cambridge Studies in Honour of C.F.D. Moule,* ed. E. Bammel, S. B. T. ser. 2, 13. London: SCM 1970. 122-34. Discusses the "I Am" sayings.

————. "The Fourth Gospel and *Religionsgeschichte,*" *Catholic Biblical Quarterly* 32 (1970) 13-24.

————. "Theology and Irony in the Fourth Gospel." In *The Word in the World (Essays in Honor of F. L. Moriarty),* ed. R. J.

Clifford and G. W. MacRae. Cambridge, Mass.: Weston College Press, 1973. Pp. 83-96.

Meeks, W., "The Man from Heaven in Johannine Sectarianism," *Journal of Biblical Literature* 91 (1972) 44-72.

Smith, D. M. "Johannine Christianity: Some Reflections on Its Character and Delineation," *New Testament Studies* 21 (1974-75) 222-48.

Talbert, C., "The Myth of a Descending-Ascending Redeemer in Mediterranean Antiquity," *New Testament Studies* 22 (1975-76) 418-40.